PRAISE FOR
THE CAREER STORIES METHOD

"In the past, your career felt like something that happened to you, rather than something you could create on purpose. Now, more than ever, we have the opportunity to shape our careers by telling the story of who we are and how we serve. Kerri Twigg has been at the forefront of this movement, helping thousands of people to reflect on how their stories shape their work. In her book, *The Career Stories Method*, she's on a mission to help more people do the work that's calling them. If that's you, then you're in good hands. This book is a great place to start building the career you want, with more intention and joy."

BERNADETTE JIWA, founder of the Right Company and creator of The Story Skills Workshop

"Kerri Twigg is quickly becoming the most trusted voice in career guidance. In this book, she outlines a simple process to find your voice and story, and chart your way to an engaging career."

DAVID BURKUS, author of *Friend of a Friend*

"Everyone needs to continually develop in their career, but most people stall because the process can be so overwhelming and hard. Kerri Twigg makes career planning fun, easy, interesting, and effective through *The Career Stories Method*. A must-read for every professional serious about career growth."

PAMELA SLIM, author of *Body of Work*

"Stories are a powerful communication tool—they amplify our beliefs and have the ability to manifest our future. That is why we must learn how to tell stories effectively. This is where *The Career Stories Method* comes in. Learn how to tell your story confidently. From branding to storytelling, Kerri Twigg is a masterful teacher and guide."

STRING NGUYEN, four-time LinkedIn Top Voice and founder of The Trusted Voice

"Kerri Twigg's *The Career Stories Method* is inspired. A respected voice in the career services industry, Kerri wants you to love yourself and your career, and gives you the tools to accomplish both. If you want more from your career, *The Career Stories Method* offers a unique blend of creativity and practicality to help you land your ideal work."

KRISTIN A. SHERRY, international bestselling author and creator of YouMap

"Yes, *The Career Stories Method* will help you market yourself in today's turbulent job market. But more importantly, it is a practice for diving deep into your psyche. Kerri Twigg's book is filled with practical activities and delivers on its promise, and in doing so helps us unlock something fundamental: Our true motivation."

ALLEN GANNETT, author of *The Creative Curve*

"Kerri Twigg is the ultimate authority on identifying the work you were born to do and landing your ideal job. She has the grit and know-how of a headhunter combined with the empathy and cheer of a best friend. *The Career Stories Method* is foolproof. Whether you want to reinvent yourself, move up a level, take a sideways step, define your 'brand,' or just take the massive cringe out of a job search, this book is a must-have."

VIV GROSKOP, author of *How to Own the Room*

THE
CAREER
STORIES
METHOD

THE
CAREER STORIES
METHOD

11 Steps to Find Your Ideal
Career—and Discover Your
Awesome Self in the Process

KERRI TWIGG

● ● **PAGE TWO** BOOKS

Some names and identifying details have been changed to protect the privacy of individuals.

Cataloguing in publication information is available from Library and Archives Canada.
ISBN 978-1-77458-061-5 (print)
ISBN 978-1-77458-026-4 (ebook)

Page Two
www.pagetwo.com

Edited by Amanda Lewis
Copyedited by Melissa Edwards
Proofread by Alison Strobel
Cover design by Fiona Lee
Interior design by Jennifer Lum

career-stories.com
#careerstoriesbook

To the people who tell stories
And the ones who listen to them

CONTENTS

INTRODUCTION

CAREERS ARE ONE of the most beautiful things you can build in your life. A career is not a job, or even a series of jobs; a career is the accumulation of your life experiences and skills. You can judge its success by how you feel in it. It's something you get to build, and, if you ignore it, it gets built for you.

I'm not a "let them build it for you" kind of person. I'm thinking you aren't one either. I can see how people become less hands-on about their career direction, and for a few years I let it happen to me.

There are three ways to kick off a career:

- You finish high school and maybe have a dreamy idea about the work you can do. If you have a dreamy idea, like I did, you might go for it.

- Or, you might decide your dream is too frivolous (usually it isn't) and you choose something safe. You stick with the safe thing because it's not too terrible.

1

- Or, you might not have a career dream at all. You take a job or go to college, then land something that pays the bills.

The job allows you to have stuff, maybe your own apartment, maybe your own mansion. But the work you do becomes about the stuff, not necessarily about how you feel as you do it. This is what people call feeling stuck. It's not that you never experience success or happiness in your career, it's more that, when you look around, you know there could be more than what you have right now.

Some people just need to make a slight shift. Perhaps you might realize that while you used to be happy working one-to-one with clients, after 15 years you don't like it anymore. Somewhere along the way your preferences changed, but the story you tell yourself, the one that goes: "I love working with clients and making every client feel cared for," doesn't match your new preference. Career happiness could be just one internal move away—like changing to a team leader role instead of a client services role. Or, moving from stuck to feeling good at work might mean big changes, like leaving an entire sector, taking courses, or starting your own business.

Whether it's a microstep or a huge leap, you only need to make 11 moves not just to land your ideal work, but also to discover your awesome self in the process. It starts with figuring out your career stories.

WHY STORIES?

Stories are a powerful force in our lives—both those we tell ourselves and those we tell others about ourselves. An unexamined one-line story could change your life.

This happened to my client Anton recently. In high school, Anton loved movies and acting. When he graduated, he didn't think he could make it in the movie business, so he took part-time jobs. After a few years, he heard graphic design could be a steady income that would still allow him to be creative. He got a graphic design certificate, landed a few graphic design jobs, and coasted. For a few years he made short videos and shared them online. He got recognition for them, and they were played on public television. A few years later, though, the site and channel where his videos were hosted was shut down. Without an audience, Anton stopped making videos.

I met Anton when he had been working as a graphic designer for many years. When he shared his career stories with me, it was obvious that his greatest joy came from making videos. Yet he wouldn't allow himself the chance to do that work. One story kept replaying in his head: "I can't make a living as a video artist." That internal story was directing his whole life.

I told him how all of the skills that kept coming up in his career stories cards (we'll get into those soon—it's the first thing you'll do) were related to video production. I said, "It sounds like you could be happy doing that work and you have the skills for it." It took time, research, story building, and testing for him to accept that he could have a career doing work he loved.

Stories—especially the ones we tell ourselves—are incredibly powerful. They can hold us back from our dreams. Or they can help us land ideal work.

The other side of stories is the ones we tell other people about ourselves. I fell into this trap. I used to hide my story when searching and applying for new jobs. I worked so hard to be the perfect candidate that I ended up "blanding in"—where you blend in so well, you become bland. Even though I was following all the advice I read in traditional job search books about how to sound professional and hit the mark, I didn't get any offers. With much hesitation, I started sharing more about my past, using my playwriting and theater background to showcase my skills and personality. I landed my ideal work.

The incredible thing about using stories to figure out your career is that you already have the source material within you. You don't need a coach or an assessment to help you figure out your career stories, you just need guidance on how to find them. This book offers that guidance.

Knowing your career stories will help you make decisions about what job to take next, and support you in asking for more money, booking more clients, and understanding yourself better.

The experience of knowing your career stories is like getting to the source of what makes you work. Your career stories are what set you apart from anyone else in your sector and company. There is an incredible power in knowing exactly what you're good at and having a story to back it up. Whether your goal is to land a new job, start a business, get promoted in your company, or become a thought leader in your industry, this method works.

As romantic as I am about stories, we need to be practical. While I would love to write a book all about finding your true calling, I'm too pragmatic. It's one thing to know your stories. It's another thing to know when and how to tell them. Part of moving through the 11 steps you are about to learn is finding and developing your stories. The other part is about how to use these same stories to build a resume or "about" page, craft interview answers, and strategize what to say to your network. It's these little, consistent, strategic moves that end up making the strongest impressions.

My aim is to help you find your career stories and give you the exact knowledge about what to do once you know them. In this book, I share approaches for using your stories to understand yourself better, write a resume, expand your network, or make more money (or any combo of these). I want to help you see and share how awesome you are.

The 11 steps I have broken this method into work best in the order I prescribe here. Each builds on the previous, and each includes a series of exercises, experiments, and self-reflections that will help you figure out and launch your career stories. Some of the steps require a lot of writing, some require a lot of thinking, and all require you to take action.

The Career Stories Method is based on four fundamental principles:

- Building an incredible career requires awareness—both self-awareness and world awareness.

- In order to gain that awareness and build an awesome career, you need to connect to yourself and others.

- Knowing and sharing your stories is the first step toward making these connections.

- The magic is in the action. It's one thing to know your stories, it's another to use them to create content, market yourself, and meet people. This is not a passive method.

This method requires effort from you. But that effort is worth it, because once you start sharing your stories with others and giving them the attention they deserve, you will start seeing and recognizing connections and opportunities that you never saw before. You won't question what ideal work looks like for you, you'll know. I've had clients call me their lucky charm. It's not that. It's that action and earnestness send a signal to the world that you're ready for something big. You are, aren't you?

This book is made for all kinds of career seekers: entrepreneurs, creatives, students, and senior-level executives in any sector. It's for people who need a job right now or are thinking about making a career move some time in the future. No matter what your goal is, the Career Stories Method is the right place to start.

STEP 1

MAKE YOUR CAREER STORIES CARDS

USED TO HAVE a difficult time knowing what my career brand was, and what type of work I wanted to do. A career brand is not a list of tasks you have done. It is a comprehensive vision of how you work and what difference you make. I kept trying to figure it out using books, assessments, and mapping tools, but always ended up in a blind alley. One day, I said, "Well, I have to use what I know. I'm going to sit here for as long as it takes to think of a way through this."

I waited 15 minutes, then an idea came to me. I'd used index cards in the past to work out scene placement when writing plays, my previous job. I thought, "Okay, index cards might help," and bought a pack of them the next day. But for a while, they sat in their pack.

A couple of days of thinking passed, and I still wasn't clear on my career brand. I took out the pack of index cards and shuffled them around, and something came to mind immediately: "That time I shared an idea with Helen about combining art-making with the existing programs. And how that idea doubled the revenue of our department that year." I wrote that story on an index card.

I knew I could trust myself to remember more moments that could serve as tiny stories about my career, skills, accomplishments, and things I am proud of. And I did. After about a week I had a small stack of filled-out index cards—and the foundation of my career brand.

You too can trust yourself to come up with solid examples of work that you are proud of. The first step in the Career Stories Method is to write one story a day onto an index card. This slow but incredibly useful method is more than what it seems to be. It asks you from the very beginning to start listening to and trusting yourself.

Sarah, a freelance brand strategist who wanted to land a corporate marketing job, called the act of collecting her career stories and writing them, by hand, onto index cards the "difference maker." Today, she tells me, "I no longer worry about what to say when someone asks me what I do. And I used to be scared of that question."

What are career stories? At this stage in the method, you simply need to think of them as stories about work you've done that made you feel alive. The days you left work feeling great about yourself and knowing you'd made a difference. Career stories can be small—like the time you stayed late the day of a snowstorm to help a woman exchange her theater seats. Or they might be huge, like the time one of my clients implemented a project management system that saved the company millions.

Your career stories cards are a tool to help you name and claim your awesome. When you are dissatisfied with your professional life, it's easy to feel lost, stuck, and unsure about where to go. You know you need a change, but the old method of just regurgitating what a job ad is asking for hasn't helped you land ideal work. This step asks you to put aside outside indicators or measures of success, and identify the moments in your career that have made your heart sing. What does your career want to be?

Here is a step-by-step guide to making your career stories cards. Get yourself a pack of index cards and a good pen. (You may even want to light a nice candle while you're at it.)

WRITE OUT ONE CAREER PRIDE STORY

Take an index card and a pen or pencil and find a space where you be can be quiet and undisturbed for about 20 minutes. Ask yourself, "What am I most proud of doing, work-wise?" or, "When was a time I felt alive at work?" If you've never had a job before, ask yourself, "What project in school did I feel delighted to be part of? What role did I play; what did I do, specifically?"

I call these "career" stories, but they don't just have to come from a job. They could come from a school project, volunteer work, teaching at Sunday School, or being on a community center board. It doesn't matter what the situation was or when it happened. Just think of a specific time when you felt very proud of the work you did.

Your first story may be small or huge. It may be about the time you improved the way a filing system worked, or when you set up an inter-office communication hub. Maybe it's the time a client called at the last minute and you stayed late to help them out. Maybe you tried a new way of listening and being led by client feedback and it grew your company from unknown to known.

The Magic of Handwriting

Why are you writing by hand? I've taught creativity workshops for nearly two decades. During workshops that involved art-making by hand, I often witness participants of various ages suddenly look up and say, "I just figured out what I'm going to do about..." after having gotten lost in the creative process.

It's especially important to write your stories by hand if you usually do everything on your phone or computer, or if you don't regularly make time for slowing down and noticing your body. Claudia Aguirre, a neuroscientist and mind-body expert, says that writing by hand is distinctly different from any other motor movement. It can increase learning and memory (you are more likely to remember the stories you write by hand), and can help you feel calm and be creative. One of the most underrated skills in career transitions is creativity—if you can't imagine your career in a new way, how can you change it?

As you consider what memory to write about for your first career story, reflect and pinpoint a specific moment when time seemed to stand still in a good way. A time that gave you an "I can't believe I get to do this work" feeling. That type of feeling comes when you are doing work you love, and that looks different for everyone. Some people feel alive when they balance an accounting report, others feel alive when they lead someone to an "aha" moment. Some feel alive when they win over a disgruntled client, and some feel alive when they get a company a grant to continue their research.

Think of moments that gave you joy, made you proud of yourself, moments where you made an impact or where you knew your work mattered, even if it was in a subtle way. You don't need to have been externally recognized for it—most of the things people are proud of never get recognition. Be honest about what work truly makes you feel alive. Your moment might be from last week, or it might be from ten years ago.

When a specific memory comes up, write down the story on an index card.

You're done for today.

KEEP WRITING ONE STORY A DAY FOR SEVEN TO TEN DAYS

Every day for the next seven to ten days, write out one story of work you loved. You will not rush ahead and write seven stories today. You will not go to your resume or past interview notes and simply re-write material from that on index cards. Every day, you will sit down and ask yourself what felt good, work-wise, when you did it, and then write down a single, specific example on an index card.

Why Seven to Ten Days?

I know that at first glance—and especially if you're already self-aware—a week to ten days feels long. Trust the process. These stories are the foundation for everything we'll be doing through the rest of the steps ahead. I've worked with job seekers who are in a rush and who say, "I don't have seven days to waste on stories, I need a job, like, yesterday." When I've hesitantly agreed to skip the process and use the first seven stories they think of in one sitting, we regret it. When rushed, the stories don't have depth, and if you try to use sub-par stories to craft a resume or career brand, it mutes the whole thing.

If you write down the same stories you have always been using—even if they've been successful in interviews or networking in the past—you're settling. It's like you've already decided what your career stories are, and you think the rest of your career should just fall into place. Career happiness doesn't come from plucking a brand out of nowhere, it comes from being honest about your skills, loves, values, and preferences. You deserve better than a dulled brand. The stories you write are the foundation of your career brand, resume, LinkedIn, and interview or networking strategies. They are the stories you'll use over and over. You dishonor your work history when you go for quickness instead of depth. The magic of this work happens by giving your stories the space they deserve.

The process needs time to form and simmer, and your stories and memories need time to rise. Sometimes you may have multiple stories coming to you every day. If you want to make a card of every one that comes up, you can, but I urge you to contain yourself to the stories that you are most proud of.

Sometimes seven days is enough time to gather your stories—this is common for people who already have a mindfulness, writing, or self-reflection practice, and are used to sitting and allowing things to come up. If you're new to writing down memories, you might benefit from taking the extra few days to create your cards. But I suggest moving to the next step after ten days, because (as you'll see) that's when the magic happens.

As you go through this step, the first few stories may come easily and feel obvious. You might write out the stories that you've been sharing for years, the one that landed you jobs or got you clients. If they come easily, do yourself and your career a favor and ask, "Did this really make me feel alive, or do I like the positive feedback I get from sharing this accomplishment?" You might find that the story really is something you're proud of, and that's great. But you might also find out it's not really something you felt good doing, or that you have outgrown the accomplishment. That's great to know. Keep working on collecting your stories.

Other stories are less obvious and may take a few days to remember. You need both the obvious and the not-obvious stories. It's rarely the obvious stories that help you figure out your next career move. If I had stuck with my first, most obvious stories, I would have come to the conclusion that I enjoyed doing the work I had always been doing. The more time you give yourself to think about what you're proud of—even if it isn't an outwardly impressive story—the more honest you'll be about what truly makes you happy at work.

Write, Don't Judge

We'll work on crafting and refining the stories later. Right now, you need to write one story a day for seven to ten days. Don't re-read them, edit them, or change them. In fact, if you're a perfectionist, tuck your written index cards into an envelope each day, and leave them all there until after the full process is finished.

Don't share your stories with anyone. Don't analyze them. Don't judge them. Trust that when you ask yourself "What am I the most proud of doing in my work?" you'll write out the answer you'll need. You will.

There is no wrong way to write your career stories. Some people worry that the stories need to be more momentous than they are. Some worry that their stories are too complicated. Don't worry about what the stories *are*; your job is to get them out on paper. Sorting, analyzing, rejecting, expanding, or tweaking them comes later. Right now you just need the material.

Your career stories cards are not meant to be written perfectly. They are for your own reference.

You can tell the judgmental part of yourself to ignore what you're doing when you're writing your stories. You can even say to yourself, "This may not look like a lot right now, and it may be all over the place. But I'm doing the work. I'm trusting this process."

It's also okay to write about work that no one else saw or gave you credit for. Anne was proud of implementing a new way to track an internal marketing process at work. "My boss didn't give me the credit for the transformation; he said it was the new manager," she said to me. "But everyone else—even the new manager—knew it was me." I told her that it didn't matter if someone else was proud of the work she wrote about in her stories. They were for her and her career development alone. Not for anyone else.

Put your judgment blinders on, and get your stories out. If your mind goes blank as you sit down to write your daily story, go to page 296 for writing prompts.

Story Specificity Matters

Ensure that all of your stories are loaded with details— that magic I keep mentioning is in those details. The more specific you can be about what work you love, the closer you can get to securing work that is meaningful to you in the future.

My client Beth had always worked in not-for-profit administration. I had asked her to do the index cards exercise, and one day she met with me in a coffee shop to talk about her stories. She laid three index cards out on the table, and all she had written on them was:

Office

Fundraiser

Meetings

She had written down the things she did at work, but not what she specifically liked about doing those things. I asked her, "Beth, tell me what you meant when you wrote 'office,'" and she told me simply that she liked working in an office. "Cool," I said. "But which part brought you the most joy?"

She looked confused. "What do you mean?" she asked.

"Think about a time you went to the office and felt great about the work you were doing," I said. "Tell me about a specific moment like that."

She thought about it, then said, "I liked to be the first one in."

I asked her to tell me more about that. "I liked getting there first thing in the morning before everyone else," she said. "I turned on the lights, made sure the coffee was ready to be brewed, opened the blinds, and checked out what needed to be done that day."

"Awesome," I said. "Can you tell me about one specific time you did this and felt proud?"

Beth told me about a day that a funder was coming in with a government minister to see a presentation about the organization. "I made sure that the large coffee pot was ready to go and the room was ready for a presentation, regular stuff," she told me. "People started arriving, but the director, Lucy, was late. Around 9:15, I went to my manager and asked where Lucy was, and she said she had called in sick. I said, 'Well ... who is doing the minister's meeting?'"

It turned out that Lucy had forgotten about the meeting. "I helped my manager quickly put together a PowerPoint presentation, found a person from our education team to help present, and had it all set up for 10 a.m.," Beth said. "The presentation went well, the minister was impressed, and our funding was increased."

"Okay," I said. "Now *that's* a story."

When you add specifics and details to your stories, your stories can work harder for you.

Saying, "I like and am proud of what I do in the office" is not as helpful as a story that has the level of detail that Beth was able to give. You don't need to write out every bit of it on your index card, but making a few notes is useful.

Later on, when you're using these stories on your resume, social media content, or networking scripts, the specific details are going to make your story irresistible. So capture them now—you'll need them.

The Different Kinds of Career Stories

Different kinds of stories are going to come up for you. They are all useful. Don't worry about how you'll use the stories yet; you just want to get them out. Some people make the error of only writing stories they think are resume worthy; please don't limit yourself like that. Your career stories cards are a place to be honest with yourself about what you truly enjoy doing.

In the beginning, you just need to capture the stories. The time to analyze and edit them comes later. If you take the full seven to ten days to get all of your stories out without judgment, you'll have plenty to work with after.

ANALYZE THE STORY CARDS

After you have written your seven to ten stories, lay the cards out on your bed or table. Choose one card and read over the story.

Now, ask yourself this: "What skill or strength did I use in this story?" Try to stay away from clichéd phrases about your work, and be as specific as possible. For example, instead of writing that you used great communication skills, define which part of communication you were great at in that moment. Was it breaking things down for people? Calming people with your voice? Writing an easy-to-understand manual? The more specific you can be, the clearer each career story will be.

When you have identified the skill or strength for a story, write it down on the other side of the card. (If you need a prompt to help you identify skills, you can find a list of example skills on page 301.)

Sometimes stories help you see that you've been selling the wrong thing. I met Mark right after he had lost a great job. On our first call, he shared that this was one of many jobs he had lost over the past five years, and he wanted to figure out a way to stop it from happening again. He was successful in all the other areas of his life: he had a great relationship with his family and he regularly enjoyed cycling, rock climbing, and meditation. It bothered him that he couldn't effectively steer his career. "I can land jobs, but I don't keep them for long. This is the one thing I wish I could figure out," he said.

I gave Mark the assignment of writing a story a day for seven days, but it was only the next day when he sent me 11 stories. They all looked like stories he had been sharing for years. They were about the sales figures he hit, the big accounts he landed, and the awards he won. These stories were surface-level impressive, but had no depth or meaning. From the outside, Mark looked like a great sales guy— despite the fact that he kept losing or quitting sales jobs.

I called Mark up and said, "These sound great, but I'd like to dig into each one of these stories deeper. Can you tell me about the specific thing you enjoyed about reaching that sales figure? Was it hitting the number? Was it closing? Was it finding the leads? Getting a bonus? The sales strategy? What about it made you feel alive?"

One of Mark's career stories cards was about a big deal he closed for a tech company. There was an important firm that his company very much wanted to work with, but they never took sales meetings. Mark told his executive team that he would get that meeting, and they told him it was impossible, but he could try. Mark approached his network to get insider information about the firm and found out the pain points they were experiencing. He meticulously put together a sales strategy, including a backgrounder on the company, key points, and words he thought the firm needed to hear. He informed the execs and the rest of his team about the plan and then put it into action, scheduling strategy sessions, training his team and executives, and doing whatever he could to see that a sales meeting was booked. The plan worked perfectly and the firm bought the software package.

In this story, Mark used a lot of skills. He used communication with peers, deep research, networking, strategy, training, identifying pain points, perseverance, project mapping, follow-through, and collaboration with multiple levels.

We wrote all of these down on the back of an index card.

Repeat the Process for Every Story

For each card and story, identify the skills you used in that specific moment and write them on the back of the index card. Some stories may have eight to ten skills associated with them, some cards will just have two or three. It's all good.

SORT THE SKILLS

Once you have identified all the skills used for each of your career stories cards, compare them. Do some skills show up more often than others? Do you have two or three that keep repeating themselves? Does one keep coming up regardless of what the story is about?

After we identified all of the skills in Mark's career stories cards, I had him look at the specifics of each story again, and search for skills he saw repeating. What showed up again and again in these moments at work that made him happy?

"To be honest," he said, "it's the research. It's researching the company so deeply that I know what they need before they say it, and I know what solution is most likely going to work for them." He added that he also liked strategizing and leading a team.

I said, "It sounds like having time to do deep research is important to you. But you also enjoy creating a plan and sharing it with others. Is work like this important in the places you have been applying to?"

Mark looked at me and said, "Shit..."

"Right?" I replied. "And when you talk with hiring people and your network, how often do you highlight that you are incredible at research, strategizing, and leading teams?"

"Never," Mark said. "I'm selling the sell."

"Sure, okay," I replied. "But are you the sell guy?"

"Nope," said Mark. "I'm a research and resource guy. Relationships too."

"Then that's the story you need to start sharing," I said. He had been sharing the story of a fast-moving closer. But that's not who he was.

We started to dig into Mark's real stories, and found a new narrative. Yes, Mark was great at closing big deals, something he had done again and again. But what made him feel alive was doing the research about a company in advance. Mark enjoyed figuring out what the biggest issues were for potential clients and knowing how the product he was selling would help them.

From there, we took some of Mark's career stories and wove them into his resume and LinkedIn profile. He started to lead networking conversations with these new stories, and eventually landed a job that needed a research-focused sales guy. Mark emailed me six months later to say that he'd already got a promotion, and he loved his new work reality. When you trust the skills your career stories highlight, you create more of the right opportunities for yourself.

When the ticket printer broke 2 hours before a sold-out show & the tech guy couldn't make it in time. Designed tickets quickly, photocopied, and handwrote ticket #s, patrons were charmed.

Design
Problem solving
Quick thinking
Thinking about audience experience
Resourcefulness (can use what I have in a new way)

DETERMINE YOUR TOP THREE SKILLS

What three skills do you see coming up most often on the back of your career stories cards? List them here:

1 _____

2 _____

3 _____

These are the skills that you love to use. These are your strategic advantage. You can use these three skills to promote yourself for your ideal work, and to assess if the job you have or want uses enough of them to make you happy. You are going to be the most satisfied and productive when you go for work that fits your skills. For Mark, it was research, putting together a plan, and sharing that plan with a team.

When I did this for myself, I noticed that, in almost every one of my career stories cards, I named the same three skills: helping others, building programs, and solving problems. This became my main career brand.

Sometimes people do this exercise and say, "The skills are all different; it doesn't work." If that happens for you, there are a few things you can do to get a clearer, more cohesive view of your top three skills:

- Double-check the wording you used for your skills on the back of your cards. Sometimes we're inconsistent in our skill labels. You might write *teaching* on one card, and *mentoring* on another, but those could be the same skill.

- Assess if the skills you identified are too general. Can you dig a bit deeper into each story and be more specific with the skills you named?

- Check if the skills are too specific or narrow in focus. For example, "knowing HR policies for every state/province" isn't a skill, it's a piece of knowledge. The skill in this instance is being well-researched, having good recall, or always being in the know.

Alternatively, sometimes people end up telling story after story of the same eight or so skills. Lucky them. If you are one of these people, look at those eight skills and choose the three you find the most interesting—the three that you would love to do the most. Having eight or more skills is perfectly possible, but that's too many to build a brand with. Narrow it down to the ones you are the most excited to have in your career.

USE YOUR SKILLS TO CREATE YOUR CAREER BRAND

Look at your list of three skills. These are the foundation of your career brand—the one cohesive story you get from all your career stories cards. You are no longer a job title. You can start seeing yourself as the combination of these three skills.

Here is the formula:

I am happiest and of most use when I am (skill 1), (skill 2), and (skill 3).

Beth's career brand is "I am happiest setting things up like meetings and events, making quick decisions to solve problems, and sharing ways to improve operations."

Mark's is "I am happiest and of the most use when I get to do deep research on hard-to-reach companies, build a strategy with that knowledge, and then lead a team to support that strategy."

Mine is: "I am happiest and of most use when I am helping others, solving problems, and building programs."

You don't have to share this formula with anyone else right now. Sit with your three skills. Pay attention to when you are doing work that makes your heart sing—if you're lucky enough to have that right now. Which of the three skills are you using? If you're in a job you hate, or you're unemployed, try looking for opportunities to use these three skills more, and see if that eases your job suffering.

You are no longer a job title, an industry, or whatever you used to say about yourself. Now you know what your favorite skills are—the ones you will use regardless of what industry, title, or role you are working within.

ACTIVITIES TO SUPPORT STEP 1

Career Stories Cards

Make your cards for seven days straight, then analyze them to identify the transferable skills.

External Connection

If you find sitting alone and thinking about your stories and skills uninspiring, talk to a current or former co-worker. Say something like, "I'm working on my career brand to make sense of the work I've done. You know me well: can you remember a time when you saw me happy at work? Did you notice what kinds of meetings or projects seemed to energize me?" Listen to what they say. Don't ask too many people; stick to just one to three. You are *not* asking them what skills they think you have—that just allows someone else to define your skills. What you *are* doing is asking them to remember when they witnessed you being energized or experiencing flow at work. (Be warned: if you work with people who never notice anything beyond themselves, you may not get what you hoped from this exercise—or you may even get answers that are misleading or counterproductive. Be mindful about who you ask, and take what you hear back with a grain of salt.)

Internal Connection

Build your connection with yourself as well. Go for a daily walk, or choose a day this week to go to a place that makes you feel creatively alive. Go to places that help you feel good, so you can write your career stories cards from a positive frame of mind. I had a client who would go for a run before he did the cards. On his run he would ask himself, "What am I the most proud of in my career?" He said the answer never came to him as he ran, but once he got home, stretched, and looked at the card, a memory would come up for him.

Ritual

Make a ritual out of collecting your stories. The story collection process is a gift to yourself. Instead of treating it like an extra to-do, can you make it enjoyable? Could you light a candle and pay attention to your breath before writing? If you're doing it with a friend or partner, could you do something before or after that makes the process feel special? I worked with a couple who asked each other, "Hey, what are you proud of doing in your career?" every night after dinner. They'd write their answers on cards and then talk the stories out. How could you make your process a delight?

Meditation

If you'd like to deepen the process—and your own self-awareness—use the story you wrote down as a way to connect with your physical body and emotions. Write out your story and tuck the card away. Sit in a comfortable position and start paying attention to what you see in the room. You may have thoughts, or hear external noises; you don't need to tune these out, but do focus your attention on what you can *see* around you. As you see each object, say its name, or simply say the word "see" out loud or silently.

Spend a few moments seeing. Then, slowly close your eyes and bring your attention to your mental screen, which is the space either in front of or behind your eyes. Pay attention to what you see there. Maybe it's gray, maybe it's swirly lines, maybe it's a clear image—whatever it is, pay attention to it. After a few more moments, bring up the memory of the story you wrote on your index card. Imagine a part of the scenario in as much detail as you can, and stretch your attention to notice how you feel as you recall the memory. Does it make you smile? Does it make your chest soften? Does it make you sit up taller? Where do you feel the memory? If any additional story details come up for you, hold on to them. Then slowly come back to the present space by opening your eyes.

Jot down any new details onto the index card. Can you remember the feeling in your body? Where do you feel career joy?

Repetition

Once you know your three favorite skills, write out your career brand for yourself every morning and night. Write the statement ten times in a notebook or on sticky notes. After a few weeks of this, you'll no longer have to go back to your career stories cards to remember your top three skills. You'll know them.

Mark would write his ("I am happiest and of the most use when I get to do deep research on hard-to-reach companies, build a strategy with that knowledge, and then lead a team to support that strategy") in a notebook every day and night. At first, he said, he felt foolish writing the line over and over again. But after a few days, he told me, "it reinforced the new brand, and I know my skills now."

Beth wrote her statement ("I am happiest setting things up like meetings and events, making quick decisions to solve problems, and sharing ways to improve operations") onto sticky notes and placed them around her house until she knew them by heart.

STEP 1 CHECK-IN

1   Did you make the seven to ten story cards and analyze them? What three skills are common among your favorite work stories?

2   Which of the suggested activities did you do? How do you feel after doing them? Did you avoid certain tasks because they made you uncomfortable? If so, could you try them now?

—

LOVE YOURSELF, LOVE YOUR CAREER

—

EACH OF US has two types of stories: the ones we tell ourselves, and the ones we tell other people.

If you're like most people, you typically focus on the external story.

What should you say to hook them? What story makes you look smart? How can you get hired with a story? But the story you tell yourself is equally important, because it has more power to hold you back.

Your internal stories are not positive affirmations—they are the stories you're living and modeling. You might say "I love myself" out loud ten times before bed every day, but then, the next day, you don't give yourself any breaks, any creativity time, any quiet time, or any reprieve from your busy life. That is you walking a different story from the one you talk. And people can tell.

This next step involves some tangible actions you can take to start living the stories you want to tell yourself. But before we dive into those actions, I invite you to first explore how you're going to take care of yourself through this process.

If a big part of feeling good at work means being aware of your feelings, then you're going to want to establish a baseline of feeling good before you even find your ideal work. This requires effort, and I strongly encourage you to do the activities that follow, along with the ones I list at the end of this step—and doing these activities is even more important if anything you read here makes you roll your eyes. Ideally, you will look back on the career exploration you are about to go through as a positive time in your life, a time you learned to listen to and understand yourself.

MAKE TIME FOR YOURSELF

Plan some monthly connection time for yourself on a regular basis. This might be a few hours or a whole day where you take yourself to a place that makes you feel alive, smart, creative, and like your best self.

For some people, that means a solo walk. For others it could be a solo trip to a flower farm, the art gallery, or even the thrift store. Whatever yours is, make sure you go alone. Don't bring your partner, kids, or dogs with you. This is time for you to reconnect with yourself. If you have the kind of life that allows it, try doing this three times a month. My self-connection dates are usually walks by the river, wandering a bookstore, or seeing a play. I always feel more energized afterward, and filled with self-appreciation. Self-connection time is especially important if you've experienced or are close to burn-out. Use this time slowly, and on your own terms. It might become your favorite day or days of the month.

For many, this is the first step in taking action in their career. If you're not claiming space for yourself outside of work, how can you do it inside of a job or with a client? The more love you show yourself now, the less suffering you will experience through the rest of this process.

PRACTICE CONTEMPLATION TO SUPPORT YOUR CAREER PLAN

People who don't have a contemplative practice have a harder time figuring out their careers, or getting a clear picture of where they are, career-wise. On my first meeting with Saul, a VP of marketing, he said, "I have a big network. I know so-and-so, and so-and-so." He wore outdated jeans and an ill-fitting polo shirt, but he sat with the confidence of a cactus—tall and untouchable, but still intriguing.

"That's great," I said. "How have these people helped you in your job search so far?"

"They haven't. I told them I was looking for a new opportunity, and heard nothing from them," he said.

"Oh, I see," I said. "It sounds like you know some people, but they aren't willing to do stuff for you. Can you tell me more about these relationships?"

Saul told me about how he had helped these guys get discounted rates on a product at his current company. He gave several more examples of helping his network in the past, and of them saying they appreciated him and would do anything for him.

I said, "It sounds like you have helped a lot of people, and when you are useful for them they appreciate it. But it doesn't sound like they know you that well, or like they're willing to do anything for you, especially if you landing a new job means they'll stop getting deals."

He thought for a moment, then nodded. "You're right, they don't really know me," he said. "They call when they're in a crisis but not at any other time. We like each other enough, but when it comes down to it, we don't know each other."

Saul spent the next few days working on an exercise I call "reality glasses." You pretend you are wearing a pair of glasses that help you see the truth. On the first day, Saul reviewed his networking list through the lens of these reality glasses, and really thought about who he was close with, and whom he did favors for. The next day, he reviewed his resume using the same frame of mind, and began to see where he undersold and oversold himself.

When we met again, he told me, "There was nothing technically wrong with my career transition plan. But it was based on a pretend scenario. I've been walking through my career with blinders on. It was hard to have this reality check, but now I know what I'm starting with based on reality, not some fantasy version of my career."

Saul asked me how he could make sure this never happened again, and I walked him through the various ways to start a contemplative practice.

CONTEMPLATE FOR CAREER CLARITY

This situation happens all the time—we're so busy doing the work that we forget to check in with what's happening in our career. That's why the next key step after uncovering your career stories is to choose a contemplative practice that you can do daily. This is the "new you" now: a human being who is aware of yourself, your stories, and your career brand. If daily feels too hard to commit to right now, try once a week to start, then increase the frequency as it becomes a habit.

Most often when people hear about contemplative practices, they think meditation or prayer. Contemplation doesn't need to be meditation, but it can include it. Contemplation is simply thinking about something deeply. You can choose your focus depending on what you need at the time. The secret to having contemplation work for you in your career is to do it daily, and deeply.

Contemplation is about getting to the source of who you are as a person and what you want to do with your life on this planet. Very few people would say they are here to just pass the time with minimal awareness.

The beauty of contemplation is that it starts out as a way to know yourself better, then becomes a life-sustaining practice. It becomes a way of life, and something you look forward to. This practice helps support you as you grow in your career, on great days and on hard days. It even helps you recognize when you're having one of those hard days. You become more aware of yourself, and of the world.

I recommend the contemplative practices that follow, and I've seen them work well for people in their career transitions. Try them all and see what feels the best to you—if it feels good as you do it, then you'll be more likely to stick with it. No type of contemplation is better than any other; all that matters is that you're doing it. The goal is to become more aware of yourself.

The more you do a contemplative practice, the better you will become at knowing yourself, your moods, your weaknesses, and your strengths. You'll spend less time seeking answers from other people or experts; instead, you'll be able to intuitively ask *yourself* smart questions. Most of the answers you need are in your heart, your bones, and your gut.

Active Contemplation

Yes, you can absolutely be doing something else at the same time—this is called active or creative contemplation. Active contemplation is where your daily practice involves movement. It could be something as free flowing or systematic as dance, or something as informal as walking. I like walking, because you can do it anywhere. Others might prefer running, yardwork, or housework. Go with the activity that works for you.

Let's say you choose walking contemplation. You might leave a bit earlier, park your car or get off the bus a little farther away than usual, and walk the rest of the way to work. As you're walking, pay attention to how your body is feeling. Count the number of times your left heel hits the ground over the entire distance. Vary the speed of your pace: how does that change how you swing your arms?

As you walk, ask yourself contemplative questions, like:

- How do I want to show up today?

- What three things am I committed to following through on today?

- What is the most unusual thing I see on this walk?

I do contemplative walks Zen-style in my hallway as a break in the afternoon. I hold my head up and walk to the end of the hall, paying great attention to when I lift my leg and how I place it back on the ground. When I reach the end of the hall, I pause, inhale, turn around, pause again, and exhale. I do this back and forth for about ten minutes, paying attention to my body as it moves. This brings me back to my body. (I admit this might be harder to do if you work in a public place, so you might have to save this one for home.)

End of day walks can be great too. You might do it right after work, after dinner, or before bed. Focus on your body, or ask yourself questions about how your day went or what you want tomorrow to look like.

Still Contemplation

This practice involves being still and silent for a period of time; often, it's a meditation.

If you've never meditated before, an easy way to get started is with an "I love myself" meditation. I developed this method after reading a quote from the Buddha that said, "Love yourself and watch—today, tomorrow, always," and I used to lead my students through it right before we did mock interviews when I taught job search strategy at the University of Winnipeg.

To start, choose a piece of music that's about six to ten minutes long and that brings you joy. Get some headphones.

Next, sit in a comfortable position—it could be in your bed, on the couch, or in a serene place outside where you won't be disturbed. Put your headphones on and play your song. As you listen to the music, start to bring your attention to your breath. Don't change the way you are breathing. Narrow your focus even more to notice when you are inhaling and when you are exhaling. Ride that for another couple of seconds. Then, as you breathe in, say to yourself, "I love myself." As you exhale, let go of whatever has come up for you. Inhale—I love myself. Exhale—let it go.

Keep doing this until the song ends.

If you like, you can extend this into an ongoing moving practice. Just say "I love myself" in your head or aloud whenever you walk through a doorway.

When I first started doing this meditation, I watched to see if anything in my life would change because of this action. And it did. I started paying attention to when I agreed to do something that didn't make me feel like I loved myself. Loving myself gave me permission to start dreaming about what else I could do. It helped me imagine an even better life.

The story you tell yourself is going to be with you through your entire career. Why not include loving yourself in that narrative?

Figuring out your next move and putting yourself out there takes a lot of courage and heart. Always make sure you're reminding yourself that this work comes from a place of love.

As time goes on, you may find you no longer need to say the words "I love myself" when you listen to your song—you may simply feel it. If that happens, listen to the song and feel the feeling of self-love. You may even progress to the point where you sit in your favorite spot without the song and simply feel self-love by paying attention to your breath.

Creative Contemplation

This practice involves creating something as part of your contemplation. That could be writing or drawing, for example.

Journaling is the most common form of creative contemplation. Some people maintain a practice in which they journal about their days and ideas. Others simply write freely in an unconscious flow. I have done "morning pages" for years—this is where you write three pages of free flow writing first thing every morning. This practice was first popularized by Julia Cameron in her book *The Artist's Way*.

Sometimes I write about how I'm feeling. Other times the focus is what I'm worried about. I've written blog ideas, short stories, and sometimes even to-do lists. I do my morning pages before anything else—especially before checking any social media or emails, because I am sensitive to other people's moods and energy. In order to protect myself daily, every morning I write and meditate and clear out my stuff before witnessing and responding to other people's stuff. This means putting my phone on airplane mode until I do my writing and meditation practices. It's like having a daily morning flight: I visit my island first, and then the islands of others.

Another way to do creative contemplation is to start a journal that you label "Operation Manual for This Awesome Human." In it, you can make lists like:

- Things that make me feel awesome
- Signs I am not loving myself
- Essential ways to care for me

Check In with a Body Scan

Get into a comfortable sitting position (you can be in a chair), straighten your spine, lengthen your neck, and relax your shoulders. Close your eyes and narrow your attention to just your body. It can be helpful to start at your toes. Get curious about your toes; send your breath to your toes.

Then, pay attention to the tops of your feet. Then your heels, then your ankles. Slowly work your way through your entire body, breathing and focusing on one part at a time.

After you've scanned your entire body, see if you can get curious about your body as a whole. You can even imagine feeling an invisible sensation one to two inches from your body.

Some people imagine seeing themselves from a bird's-eye view; others sense their body by feeling all the sensations from the inside. Whatever works for you is best for you. As you focus on your body, you're likely to experience one part wanting extra attention, usually through a pang, an itch, or an even subtler sensation. Focus in and pay attention to that feeling— then, as the sensation fades, bring your attention back to sensing your body as a whole, focusing in and out of sensations as they arise.

Stay with this feeling and relax. Or, try processing rejections or setbacks you've experienced.

You might see it as words, or you might hear it as a voice—just remember the rejection you got. Then, return your awareness to your body. Do you feel the rejection or setback anywhere specific? Can you locate it?

Many feel rejection in the pit of their stomach. Some feel it in their throat or chest. Locate the sensation and, instead of talking about it, judging it, or giving it more power, feel the feeling and say to yourself, either aloud or in your head, "feel." Then just keep doing that: breathing into it, and naming it "feel." That's all it is. Just a feeling.

As you do your job search, any time you feel emotional about a rejection or a misunderstanding, return to this meditation.

You are not denying the emotion or experience. You are simple saying, "I feel this. I feel rejection in this space in my body. It is a feeling." That way, you don't let that feeling have more power than it deserves in your life. And you don't allow it to stop you from going for your dreams. You can handle rejection.

Connective Contemplation

This practice involves sharing your thoughts and ideas with others. It could be through a formal support group or something more casual. This works great for people who need external accountability to follow through on things.

Sometimes it's hard to see things for yourself, so having a group of people to share with can be helpful. This could be a meditation group, a self-help group, or a group of job seekers or career explorers. You simply all commit to some sort of daily practice, like meditating or journaling. Each week might have a theme. Then, once or twice a month, you share your experience with the group, while listening to theirs in return. You can keep your own daily practice, but you also get the release of sharing, and the benefit of feedback from others who might see or hear things you don't.

KNOW YOURSELF, KNOW YOUR CAREER

A large part of enjoying your work is knowing yourself and your career. The most common thing that happens to people in their careers is that they unknowingly check out. Days blend together, weeks and months go by, then you look around and say, "What have I been doing? What am I even doing with my life?" This happens when you aren't present. The beautiful moments in life are not just the vacations, births, ceremonies—it's the little day-to-day stuff. If you've been ignoring that, it's hard to have a meaningful career. Annie Dillard is right: "How we spend our days is how we spend our lives."

When you don't like your day-to-day reality, it's easy to check out. It's easy to think that things like trips, new clothes, or gadgets are going to fill that hole. They don't. Sometimes it makes the gap even bigger because you're overspending to feel better, then you need to make more money to fill the gap. The way around this is investing effort in a contemplative practice. This can look like so many things, but it boils down to this: you're committing to doing something that helps you be more present.

Being more present makes you a better connector. Beyond helping you know yourself better, a contemplative practice can help you develop skills that make you an incredible person to network with. Contemplation moves you from always being inside your head to starting to notice what else exists. You'll notice that as you take better care of your inner self, your outer self becomes more relaxed. When you arrive at a networking event, you love yourself, so you don't overcompensate. You're more aware of other people, their faces and their feelings.

A big part of loving yourself is being honest with yourself and accepting what you're working with. Where you are is just fine. It's okay to want something else, but start by accepting what is. You'll get there in your own way. You always do. While contemplation may seem selfish at first, once you do this work and start to love, accept, and understand yourself, you'll be in a better place to accept and understand others.

ACTIVITIES TO SUPPORT STEP 2

Personal Connection Day

Open your calendar and plan what day you'll do something you love alone. Block off that time. It's precious. While you're at it, block off a day every month for the next three months.

Daily Practice

Choose a contemplative practice to support your daily energy and reflection. If you're new to this, try a new one every day and see which style works best for you.

Manual for Yourself

Get a new notebook and name it "Operation Manual for This Awesome Human." Fill it with affirmations, the skills from your career stories cards, notes on what a dream job feels like. Then, add in some basic advice on how to take care of yourself. For example, mine has tips like this: "If you're snapping at your family, stop. Drink water. Go for a walk."

Journaling

Start doing daily gratitude journaling. Commit to writing out three or more things you are grateful for each day.

Connective Contemplation

If you know you do best when you're able to share your experiences with people, find or start a group to meet up for mindfulness exercises or sharing. This could done in person or online.

STEP 2 CHECK-IN

1   Did you plan and do a personal connection day? How did it feel? If you didn't do it, start to plan what you'll do next month.

2   Which of the suggested activities did you do? How did you feel after doing them? Did you avoid certain tasks because they made you uncomfortable? If so, could you try them now?

—

FIND WORK
THAT MAKES YOUR
HEART SING

—

I T'S POWERFUL TO know what skills you want to be using most often in your daily work. But it doesn't answer the question of why that works matters, or where you should use those skills. This step is about figuring out your career values. This requires dreaming and being practical.

Gary, a project manager with a corporate real estate firm, said he felt "stuck and under immense pressure." Early on in his career he had success. "Right after college, I got this job and had some early wins. So I bought a condo. I kept getting promotion after promotion, until I became the head guy at our firm. Everything went through me," he said. "Everyone I graduated with has incredible titles at great companies, and they're happy. But I feel like I'm drowning."

We talked about the work that made him feel alive, and every story he told included him leading a team. "But the big companies don't pay people to be working alongside a team, they pay guys like me to think and strategize," he said. I asked him, "What if you could find a company that allowed you to advise and be in the C-suite, because you're great at that, but also encouraged you to be with the team?"

He said that would be perfect. "Cool," I said. "Let's get even more specific about the work you'd get to do, and what it might look like."

Many of the jobs that exist today didn't exist ten years ago. One of the remarkable things that changed work during the COVID-19 pandemic was how many brand-new roles were created. I saw companies like Shopify put out job ads without an official title, instead only describing the work to be done. This will continue. If you hold on to an outdated and safe story of yourself and the work that you can land, you'll be left behind in the future of work.

Just because a job doesn't exist right now, that doesn't mean it won't one day. You can create ideal work for yourself once you know what it looks like. There are two parts to identifying ideal work: your values and the fit. In this step, we'll explore your values.

PUT YOUR VALUES INTO ACTION

Values are huge in career exploration, and you may not know it until you're working in a place that doesn't value the same things you do.

We can all do great work. We are all capable of contributing to companies, making things happen for people, improving systems, and being employee superstars. The thing about being an employee superstar is that we might be happy at first, but if the work doesn't match our values and desired life, we won't be for long.

There are three values that everyone should reflect on in relation to their career: money, status, and making a difference.

Let's Talk about Money, Honey...

One of the reasons we work is to earn money. Money issues come up in funny ways during career transitions. Some clients have it all figured out and don't care what they make. Others care too much, and some don't want to talk about money at all. But since most of us work to earn money, it needs to be a part of your career decision.

When I lead career development workshops, I ask the participants to get out a piece of paper and draw a long line. I tell them to label one end of the line 0 and the other end of the line 10. Then I ask a question: "On a scale from zero to ten, how important is money to you in your career?" Without fail, someone always yells out "Ten, of course!" and the class laughs. I say, "It may be ten for you, but for some people in this room it might be a one or a five. The important part is knowing where you stand, because your career story is going to look different depending on what you value."

Do this exercise yourself by marking your answer on the line below.

0 ————————————————————————— 10

Be honest about how important money is in your life. There's a difference between the way you show up in a money-important career and a non-money-important career. In my workshops, someone will usually say, "What if money is important, but so is helping people?" That's fine. There's nothing wrong with money being important to you. I see people hurt themselves by saying it's not important when it is. They accept low-paying jobs where they get to make a difference, but end up leaving after one to three years because of burn-out and salary dissatisfaction. Then they'll apply for low-salary jobs again, and continue the cycle.

On the other end, some people will say ten, but when we get down to it, they're really at a five. They want to make a decent salary, afford to buy whatever they want at the grocery store, and go on a trip or two every year. They live within their means, get some down time, and make a difference. When a person who would be happy at a five searches like someone who needs a ten, it negatively affects them. They often don't want the lifestyle, work ethic, and stress that comes with a ten. I've worked with people who were unhappy making $350,000 a year. Then, by owning this process, they learned to take jobs that paid $200,000 and felt a lot happier. So be honest.

Money is one of the most complicated stories that humans tell themselves. If you're not honest about how important money is to you, you will make poor career decisions— ones that don't fit with your values. You'll take work that pays you too little because you feel uncomfortable asking for more money. Or you'll do work that exhausts you and makes you cranky with your family and friends, but pays you very well.

I once worked with Jay, who listed money as one of their top three values.

Coming to this realization was eye-opening for Jay, because for 15 years they had applied for and accepted roles in the IT sector that underpaid them. They had a fantastic reputation in the local market and were never out of work. In their spare time, they made IT tutorial videos for YouTube that received great feedback. They had positive performance reviews, and from the outside everything looked great. But they couldn't afford the things they wanted in life—specifically, home ownership and more spare time for personal pursuits and holidays. After a long career, they were still getting the minimum vacation time.

After they explored their relationship with money and the other values, they were able to admit that money was important. They stopped applying for low-salary positions, and started to present themselves as the expert they were. Soon, they landed a job that paid $25,000 more a year, doing more or less the same thing they were doing before.

"Knowing that money was important to my career stopped me from underselling myself," they told me. "My mom said that the most important thing at work was a job well done, but that's not the case for me. It's a job well done and fairly paid." Jay got the best of both worlds by getting a job that paid well, but that also allowed the time and energy it took to continue making YouTube videos.

Money can be important to you and you still might be doing work that doesn't pay awesome right now. Some career paths require a few years at a less-than-stellar salary in order to build up your reputation and experience. If this reflects your career journey, don't put aside that knowledge that money is important to you. Keeping that front of mind will allow you to give an enthusiastic "yes" when you're asked to do extra work, take on additional responsibilities, or go beyond your job description. At the same time, where appropriate, it will allow you to negotiate how these extra tasks will be compensated.

I learned this one the hard way. As a people pleaser, for years I would say yes to every additional task without complaint. I would respond with great eagerness and enthusiasm, even if the new work negatively affected my home life. I thought I was showing management that I was a team player, but I was actually doing the opposite. What I was actually showing my company was that I would do all that extra stuff without it costing them a thing. So, instead of promoting me when new roles opened up, they kept me in the same role. I was told I didn't have leadership qualities, since I had proven to them for years that I was happy to follow along, no matter the cost.

Status Matters

Status matters in career decisions. Alice was a burned-out executive director. She said, "Kerri, I just want a role where I don't have to take any work home. Something simple: I just show up, do my work, and don't have to make any decisions."

All of Alice's career stories, however, were focused on making big decisions, leading large organizations through major changes and acquisitions, and creating multi-year plans. She was used to being in charge, calling the shots, and moving things forward.

At one point, she took a two-month leave of absence from her ED role and was bored within a week. She started volunteering a few hours a week at a local women's not-for-profit group. As you can guess, within three weeks she had assessed the operation, scheduled a meeting with the center's ED, and started writing a proposal to improve the kitchen area. I laughed when she told me this. "It sounds like no matter where you go, whether you're the boss or not, you can't help but become the boss," I said. She laughed too, and admitted, "I like to lead."

We revisited her initial desire to take on a low-responsibility role. I said it was rare to have a such a low-power role but still be able to lead things. Once she saw that she cared about status, her career plan changed. She took her career stories and opened a business that used her favorite skills, consulting for companies as they acquired new businesses and initiated major change. We worked out how to position her stories to build trust with her client companies. She let her network know she was available, built up her website, and launched her business. Alice started with a small contract, and within a year was making more money doing work she loved. And she was in control of her workload.

Alice changed her personal story of "I don't want to work hard," because it was only based on her not knowing what to do next. Her new brand became "I like to make decisions and lead organizations through major changes." That reframing allowed her to own and trust her decision, and her story.

Whatever status rung makes you happiest is the one you should go for. Some people are content to do their work behind the scenes. Others like to lead, but also do the work alongside colleagues in similar positions. Some people like to plan and then dictate what the next move is. Status matters.

If you truly love to run workshops where you act and feel like an equal to the participants, be honest about that. If you love to lecture but prefer to be seen as the untouchable expert, be honest about that. Honesty allows you to be extra clear with other people about where you fit best.

Sometimes when an entrepreneur starts out, they're simply happy to have their business and their customers, and they don't think about status. I worked with one client, Noelle, who transitioned from working as an in-house editor at a small publishing house to working as a freelance editor for businesses. In the early days, she said, "Status doesn't matter to me. As long as I'm making money editing, and I have flexibility, it's cool." But within a year of freelancing, she said, "Oh, the status thing matters after all."

Noelle had a good reputation and got a lot of corporate clients and editing work. Some clients treated her like they were doing her a favor by hiring her. Others respected her ideas and work. After a year, she changed the way she spoke about her work to potential clients before she began working with them, to ensure that they would give her the status she needed.

Every human is valuable. And every job is important. One title having more status than another doesn't make that role more important. At the same time, though, status is likely going to make a difference in how you feel. It matters both that you love and are proud of the work you are doing *and* that you feel respected and seen in the workplace at a level that suits you. So be honest about it. How important is it to you that you get recognition for your work? How important is having a big title?

Making a Difference at Work

I often hear, "I want to make a difference." So do I.

Making a difference does not mean you have to work for a charity or not-for-profit. You can make a difference anywhere.

It's good to know what difference you want to make in the world and how you want to make it. Some people are happy to have a career that allows them nice things: they can buy a car, a cottage, and donate the rest. They don't need their jobs to make a difference for a lot of people, just for people in their company or community.

Others need to make a difference in the larger world, and to be able to see that difference. They don't want to just donate to a cause, they want to be the one doing the work for that cause.

Sometimes people lose sight of how important making a difference is to their career, or they don't notice when their work loses its meaning. This happens to both company employees and to entrepreneurs. If you have success in your career, especially early success, that can attract growth thinkers to you and your work. Growth thinkers are people who always want to make things bigger. They're not inherently bad—growth can be great. But not everything needs to get huge.

I was working with a business marketing coach, Kylie, who had success in her first three business years. She worked one-on-one with clients, ran a few online workshops, and traveled three times a year to speak at conferences. We had planned her business moves to match with her skills and values, and it was paying off. I hadn't spoken with her for a while, and one day I noticed that she was running a new training program with some other coaches. I messaged her to say congrats on the growth, and Kylie replied with: "Help!"

Kylie had caught growth fever, which makes you think that you haven't achieved enough when you have. Anyone can catch growth fever. I spoke to Kylie and she explained that, because her business was going so well, a lot of people had reached out and offered to help her scale. She started working with a company that promised growth through list-sharing, but it required her to sell her clients a package that bundled her coaching services with those of others. Kylie told me she was expected to bring in a certain number of leads, and to share the program with her list. Her former clients and followers were turned off by the new offer and stopped following her. "In an effort to scale

I ended up building a business I don't like and that helps fewer people," she said. "I've pissed off the people that I would like to work with and now I have clients who think I'm someone else by how I've been acting."

So, she went back to Step 1. She created her career stories cards from scratch, and identified the three things she offers that bring her career joy. Kylie checked in with her values and saw that the new program was not a match with her money values (she was making less than before now), her status values (she preferred to be subtle and behind the scenes, working one-on-one to make a difference), or for fit (the work had the wrong partners and attracted ill-fitting clients). After eight months of intentional action, Kylie was finally able to return to her former business model, this time feeling even clearer about who she was and how she made a difference.

This can happen with employees too. So often I hear about a person who had exceeded expectations at an entry-level job and so got promoted to management. Then they do amazing work as a manager, and believe they'll be even happier as an executive. They work hard for years and finally land the executive role, only to find it an ill fit. They lose sense of the difference they were trying to make.

A strong and satisfying career comes when you're honest about how big or small you want your work to be, and fine-tune your actions to match. In his book *Company of One*, Paul Jarvis talks about how he intentionally kept his business small. It's an inspiring read on how small can still have impact. If you're staying small because that's where you think you can make the biggest difference, embrace it. If you're staying small because of fear, build in baby steps to test out growth.

What Are Your Personal Values?

Money, status, and making a difference are three of the most important values to understand your relationship with, and I encourage every person to examine where they sit with them because they affect how successful you feel. But there are also other more personal values that are important to consider, and these will be specific just to you.

Jill, a data analyst who wanted to move from working in startups to a larger corporation, told me her top three work values were honesty, freedom, and autonomy. I asked what she meant by these things, because everyone interprets such values differently. I might see freedom as being able to run a project how I like, and someone else might see freedom as having flexible hours at work.

Jill said, "Honesty in my career means that I need to work with people who do what they say and say what they do. I need to trust my co-workers. Freedom means that I don't want to be assessed by the hours I work. If I'm deep into a project and want to stay up until midnight because I get into the groove of it, I

don't want to have to be in at 9 a.m. I don't need complete flexibility, but I need the freedom to flex the way
I work. And by autonomy, I mean that I need a place
where I have a voice and get to decide the best way to
work with the data."

When I work with people, I usually ask, "What values
are important to you?"—and often they immediately
know the answer. You don't need a quiz or a list of values to figure this out; you already know it for yourself.

Doing the work to uncover and understand your own
values is critical, but knowing your values and acting on
them are different arenas. Once you acknowledge your values, you need to think about how you model those values
in your career. One way to define how you do this—and to
guide your actions and decisions in the future—is to add
your values to your career brand.

If you remember Beth, her brand became "I am happiest setting things up like meetings and events, making
quick decisions to solve problems, and sharing ways to
improve operations. I value respect, open communication,
and order."

Mark's was "I am happiest and of the most use when
I get to do deep research on hard-to-reach companies,
build a strategy with that knowledge, and then lead a
team to support the strategy. I value depth, autonomy,
and integrity."

Once you know your values, like Beth and Mark did, you can add to them to your career story.

ACTIVITIES TO SUPPORT STEP 3

Money Line

If you haven't done this exercise yet, do it now. Draw a line and label it 0 to 10. Ask yourself: "How important is money in my career?" Be honest. How is your current work helping you realize where you want to be on that line?

Personal Money Story

Do some journaling to explore the story you tell yourself about money. Use these prompts:

- How much money do I need to earn to keep living my current lifestyle?

- What type of lifestyle do I aspire to, and what level of income do I need to support it?

- What would I most like to change about my attitude toward money?

- Is my current lifestyle about impressing someone else, or impressing myself?

- Is it my salary or my saving/spending habits that are contributing to my current financial situation?

- If I found a position that paid a lot more than I currently make, how would that change things for me?

Status Graph

Draw a graph where the bottom is 0 and 10 is the top. Think about all the roles you had in your career so far. Plot a line that shows what status level your role was supposed to have; for example, if you were hired to be a receptionist at a law firm, it might be seen as a two or three.

Next, in a different color, plot out how much status you had when you were in that role. For example, I was the receptionist once at a radio station, but because I volunteered to do extra work like accounting, radio traffic programming, and marketing assistance, my status was a six.

How do your roles compare? Do you tend to stay in line with what they ask for? Or do you move to a higher or lower status to feel more comfortable?

Two Objects Game

Grab two objects. One represents how you currently make a difference in your career. The second represents the difference you *want* to make in your career. Write out a story about how close are you to making the right amount of difference in your career. Do you need to take a step back? Take more actions? Or keep contributing at the same level?

Circle of Difference

Draw two circles, one around the other. In the inner circle, write down the names of all the people who affect your current day-to-day and community work. In the outer circle, list the people who are affected by the things you make or do; this could be an end customer or a supplier, for example. Whose world do you affect even if you rarely or never see them?

Examine your two circles and think about how far you want your impact to go. Are there any people you'd like to influence that you currently don't? Take a pen in a different color and write those names down. Are there people whose lives you affect, but you don't want to anymore? A group of people or a sector that you wish to leave? Cross those names out. Do you need to add a third circle because you want to make an even wider difference, perhaps including animals or communities or the environment? How wide is your new circle? Draw it out and add in all the names.

This chart shows you how much of a difference you want to make, and where you want to make it. Look for work that allows you to have this kind of impact.

Top Values List

It's worth knowing what other values are important to you. Some people easily know their values—if you don't, look at the list of values on page 302. Select your top five and list them in order of importance.

Knowing your values and acting within them are two different things. Review your list and reflect on how you model these in your life. If you don't model them as fully as you'd like to at work, write out specific actions you'll take to be living more in line with what you value.

STEP 3 CHECK-IN

1   Are you more aware of your values now? Do you believe that you could land work that hits all your values? What is your plan for assessing whether an organization is a match with your values?

2   Which of the suggested activities did you do? How did you feel after doing them? Did you avoid certain tasks because they made you uncomfortable? If so, could you try them now?

FIND AND MAKE
THE PERFECT WORK
ENVIRONMENT

FIT IS HOW your work values and attitude match the culture of an organization. Culture can be about the physical space and how you work, but it mainly comes down to a few areas: people, management/reporting style, work style, and spirituality at work.

I've been involved in hundreds of outplacement meetings, in which a company hires me to help them let someone go. While sometimes it has to do with restructuring or shutting down operations, in most cases the reason people lose their job is fit. The manager will say something like, "Ted is incredible at his work, and technically there's nothing wrong with him—he just doesn't fit."

Not fitting means his work style, attitude, and/or personality clash with the culture of the company. In some cases, HR will work with people who don't fit to help them understand how they can adapt their behavior. Sometimes this works. Sometimes it works for a short while, and then a big clash comes.

It hurts to lose work over fit. A company is really saying that your personal style is wrong for them. The other side of that coin is that the company's culture may be wrong for you.

Fit matters in running your own business too. Solo biz owners love to share the benefits of working for yourself, including making your own hours, choosing what work you get to do, and being selective about your clients. You can absolutely start a business for yourself that you hate—I see it often enough. Most commonly, I see people decide to start a coaching business, then learn that they hate working alone and having to market themselves. If you know what fit is best for you before you build a business, you have a better chance of building something you want to stay in.

I was working with a client, Gurpreet, who did not fit with her current company. She had worked for a marketing agency for over seven years in multiple roles. She got moved from role to role and kept being told that she needed to be "less bossy and assertive." She tried, but she couldn't help but direct people to do their work better. When we first met, she did her career stories cards and found that her favorite work, even though management didn't always like it, had three qualities:

- Improving processes

- Doing deep research into where and why an inefficiency was happening

- Having conversations with the team to help them deal with change

While technically her job title included all three of these things, she worked for a company that said it wanted innovation, but also resisted it. To add to the stress, there was a new executive team who wanted to hold off on any changes until they got their bearings. Gurpreet brought forward simple changes to improve minor procedures and was told to wait. She had been waiting for eight months as morale dipped, and she was getting tired of it.

There are always times in our work when we are prevented from using our favorite skills. Sometimes we need to wait until the next quarter to start our dream project. Other times there is a lot of pre-work that needs to happen before we can start, but it's worth it when we get to do the work. In Gurpreet's case, she was never going to be able to do work she wanted to do with that company. She loved the people. She loved the clients. She loved the company product and reputation. But it wasn't the right fit for her.

Before Gurpreet quit her job and randomly applied for new roles, she needed to figure out what kind of place she wanted to work at, which industry she preferred, whether she wanted to work for herself or someone else, and what the ideal culture would be for her.

UNDERSTAND THAT FIT MATTERS

You can land a job doing work that you love, but if you don't fit with the people, philosophy, and culture, you won't be happy. This happens often with people who generally get along with everyone. They can flex that get-along muscle and swallow things longer than most, but they eventually burn out. It's not that you need to like every co-worker and all the office art, but it helps if you like most of it. Some of us can't pretend, right from the beginning. I have a friend who cannot, no matter how she tries, hide her true feelings. Luckily she works remotely, and she likes the philosophy of the company.

When we craft our stories we always start with what work we love, because that's the core piece we need. Then we take one step outward and imagine what that next move could be. This involves a balance between dreaming and being practical. At this point in the process, you don't need to make a decision about what to do next; that's two steps away. Right now, you're going to give yourself permission to imagine "what if," but you'll base that "what if" on the skills you identified in Step 1, when you wrote your career stories cards.

Remember, the work that makes you happiest, that you can't help but do, that makes your job worth doing, is the work you want to fill your career with. This is the work that draws on the skills in your stories. Now, you want to dip into exploring where to best use those skills.

FIND YOUR RIGHT PEOPLE

There's a saying that goes, "People don't leave companies, they leave bad managers," and it's true. When I talk with potential clients, the call often starts with, "I love my company, I've been here for years, but recently there was a change in management and now everything is different."

Entrepreneurs say the same thing. "I think I need to rebrand. I used to get incredible clients, but lately the teams I've been asked to work with are so draining. I didn't build a business to feel tired like this."

It makes a difference who you work with. I was once a programs officer with the government, doing work that wasn't right for me. My co-workers made it enjoyable— they were smart, innovative, kind people who got things done. I stayed a year longer than I wanted to because of those great co-workers. I've also worked for companies where I enjoyed the work and used my ideal skills, but the people made the experience awful.

Knowing your right people goes beyond your co-workers; it's also knowing your ideal clients. This, more than any other category, can change without you even being aware of it. Nadia had a PhD in epidemiology and her work was mainly within government. She ran research programs and had built a strong reputation in her field. She took five years off to adopt and raise a child. During her time away from government, she took on volunteer roles with the community to help share information about the health needs of children, her specialty. When Nadia decided to return to work, she landed a job quickly based on her past performance within the government.

Nadia called me after a few months and said, "It's weird. It's like the work has lost its meaning. I used to love influencing policies and being on task forces, but now it feels constrictive to me."

We examined Nadia's career stories and noticed that much of her career joy was working with community women to solve everyday issues. At first, Nadia's concern was about taking a deep salary cut. We looked for alternative places where her experience and skills could be valued and where she could work with her ideal clients. Her career brand changed from "I am best when helping to inform policies that affect public health" to "I am best when I am working alongside people to collect child health information through interviews and education." It took a few months, but Nadia landed a new director role, where she partly worked with community members and organizations, but also made policy recommendations to the government.

Nadia had changed. Her ideal people had changed.

If you find yourself not looking forward to work, the job might be right, but you might not be able to serve your ideal people. It's worthwhile checking in to see that you are doing work for your ideal client.

DETERMINE YOUR PREFERRED MANAGEMENT/REPORTING STYLE

How your boss or the executive team manages you is often overlooked, but it makes a huge difference to your career success. If your preferred style of working is casual but you land a job with a micromanager, you won't be happy even if you get to do work you love and you admire the company.

Matt, for example, wanted to work in the cannabis industry. He saw a posting for a government minister's assistant for cannabis legislation and said, "This is my dream job." I said, "I don't think it is." While it was a great-paying job in the cannabis field, it would require him to follow strict protocols, react slowly to change, and write a lot of reports. All of his career stories were about innovation, breaking barriers, and making things happen. He moved forward with applying for the job anyway and he made it to the second interview. For that round, he needed to write a government memo following a strict format and create a mock presentation using a pre-set template. As Matt was creating the presentation, he decided to mix up the formats and add in some extra zip. I told him that these actions would prevent him from landing the job. He ignored my advice and did it his way. He didn't get the job—his interviewers told him that while he had the right skills, they were concerned about his ability to prosper in the role.

Be honest with yourself about how you like to be managed, and seek out work that brings out the best in you.

This can be part of your career brand. For Matt, his went from "I'm an innovative cannabis advocate who makes things happen with few resources" to "I'm an innovative cannabis advocate who makes things happen with few resources and a lot of freedom."

DETERMINE YOUR
PREFERRED WORK STYLE

Just as you need to be clear on your management style, you want to be clear on your work style as well. Think back to a time when you were productive. What circumstances allowed that? If you do your best work alone in an office with the door closed, look for work that gives you that private time.

If you take a job that requires constant collaboration, you might be fine in the beginning, but after a few months you'll find yourself looking for reasons to work from home, or seeking out other space in the building. Yes, we can all adapt and learn new skills, but honor your natural learning and work style. If ignored, these are the things that end up draining people.

DETERMINE YOUR
IDEAL WORK ENVIRONMENT

Beyond the people you work with and for and beyond how you do the work, consider your work environment itself. Aaron had spent his entire career in theater as a set technician. He never dressed up for work; he worked long hours for some parts of the year, and few hours at other times. He preferred a casual environment. After years of working in theater, Aaron realized he loved to organize people, and decided to study project management. "At the theater," he said, "while everyone else just wanted to start building the set and props, my favorite part was that first meeting where we laid out the timeline and deliverables."

He told me a story that exemplified that interest: "One day, the production manager had a bad reaction to a bee sting. He called from the hospital and asked if I could lead the production meeting for him. I wasn't sure I could, but I did it anyway. I loved it—I set everything out super clear, answered all the questions from the builders and tech people, and it felt right, you know?"

Aaron found his skills. While he loved theater, what he enjoyed doing the most was managing projects and people. He got his project management certificate and started to apply for jobs. But while he was landing interviews, he never landed the job. That's when he called me again.

Aaron told me where he had been applying and I said, "You know, some of these places are ideal in the work you would do, but they're not the ideal environment for your style. You'd have to wear a suit to this one, and this one has a lot of report writing and has you outside all of the time." We made a checklist of ideal environments, and he used that list to land a project management job at a window company. "It's a lot like theater," he told me. "We're building and shipping all the time, it's just that the show is not public."

Defining the Work You Love

One of the biggest struggles in a job search is determining if you will like a particular job and what you will be doing in it. In Step 1, I offered you a formula for determining your career brand. Now I'd like to show you one that can help you uncover the right kind of work. It looks like this:

The work you enjoy + your values +
your ideal work environment = your ideal role.

Here's how this would apply to two of the people you've met so far:

Beth: "I am happiest setting things up like meetings and events, making quick decisions to solve problems, and sharing ways to improve operations. I value respect, open communication, and order. I do this work well with a manager who I get to meet with regularly and in a casual office setting."

Mark: "I am happiest and of the most use when I get to do deep research on hard-to-reach companies, build a strategy with that knowledge, then lead a team to support the strategy. I value depth, autonomy, and integrity. I prefer my manager to treat me like a peer, and I'm better at knowing a goal and how to get it, rather than being told what to do. I like to wear a suit to work."

This is not a statement you need to share with anyone—it can sound a bit awkward. But it will give you career clarity. This formula can help you know what to look for in ideal work, and keep you on track until you find it.

EXPLORE THE ROLE OF SPIRITUALITY IN YOUR WORK

Some people see work as separate from their life's purpose. Others see it as an expression of their purpose—if you are one of these people, you need to bring your soul to work. I'm not necessarily talking about the role of God in your work, but it might include that for you.

Ask yourself this: Do you think the work you do is a spiritual expression? Do you think it's an extension of creative energy of the universe? If you get a big "no" feeling from that, cool. If the idea piques your curiosity, I encourage you to think about it longer.

I bring this up because, as a teacher and coach, I'll talk to people about their work and they'll say things like, "I don't know why I'm drawn to this work, or why I have this skill. But when I do it, I feel like it's a higher expression of myself, like it's not even me doing the work anymore. Maybe like a religious experience, except I'm just coding programs, you know?" And I'll say, "Yes, I know."

I think careers can include mystical experiences. And the more my clients embrace and follow that feeling, the more career happiness they feel. You don't need to start believing in God or another higher power for this feeling to happen. It's about listening. When you get really great at listening to yourself and taking action on your big dreams, things start to happen. My clients call them miracles. Take what happened to these clients, for example.

Sophie loses her job but is terrified to tell her mother about it. Sophie's mom has a heart condition and she doesn't want to worry her. Her job search goes on longer than expected, making her anxiety about her mother finding out grow worse. Finally, Sophie tells her mom the truth. Her mom listens, then says, "I was just talking to Sue down the street, whose employee quit. They're looking for someone who does account management like you. I'll call." Sophie lands ideal work, finds a home closer to her new office, and gets to live closer to her mom.

Patrick spends six months applying for jobs and not getting a single interview. We spend two sessions getting his career brand right, then he runs into an old friend at a coffee shop and is introduced to their partner. The couple asks Patrick what he is working on now and he uses his new career brand to introduce his work. He finds out

the friend's partner is the director at his dream company
and he lands the job.

Janessa reluctantly reaches out to her ideal company to
do an informational interview, and is offered a job interview on the spot.

These are all examples of people listening to themselves,
putting in the work, taking action, and having the universe
reward them for it. It could be called being prepared, syn-
chronicity, luck, or magic—it's up to you.

There is no right answer to the spirituality question. If
you think about this and discover that your daily work may
need to have a spiritual aspect, trust that feeling. Really
trust it. It's unlikely that you'll be happy at work if it doesn't
have deep meaning to you.

If, on the other hand, you discover that you don't need
your job to be part of a higher expression of yourself, cool.
You can still have an incredible, meaningful career and be
joyful at work. But it does mean that the true joy of your
life is outside of work. So be sure to leave time for that stuff,
whatever it is for you.

I'm the type of person who needs my work to be an
expression of my highest value, creativity, and soul. I'm
made that way. When I've been in jobs where my creativity, love of human connection, and joy in building new
projects were not respected, I felt like I was suffocating. It
de-energized me and I became an underperformer.

I have friends and family who hold jobs that don't allow them to be creative or build new things, and they're fine. They go to work, they do their tasks, they help out and make a difference. That lack of creativity in their day-to-day work doesn't make them feel like they are suffocating at all. It's good to know which way you lean.

ACTIVITIES TO SUPPORT STEP 4

Your Ideal Team

A big part of being happy at work is knowing what kind of people you do your best work with. This includes your boss, clients, co-workers, and partners. Answer the following questions:

What do I like the most about my most recent boss?

_____

What do I like the least about my most recent boss?

_____

What have I learned from my most recent boss?

_____

I had the best experience working with people who...

_____

Team Reflection

Journal about the people you do your best work with. Do you need to work with experts? Type As? Casual, light-hearted, responsible people?

Your Ideal Job Description

Imagine that the recruitment field has completely changed and the way to get jobs now is that candidates have to write the job description themselves. Write a job advertisement that shares who you are and what you value in life. You can include your skills, passions, values, personality, and desired salary.

_____

_____

_____

_____

_____

_____

Career Map

Grab a piece of paper, some pencils (colored markers and/or paint can be fun too!) and draw a map of your career so far. It can take any form: it could be a circle, a long line, random lines, a maze... it doesn't matter. I usually draw each job as a circle, then join them with a line. As you look at the jobs you have had, reflect on what you loved, what you hated, and why you left. This will reveals patterns to you: what you have done, the kind of people you work well with, what you are good at, and what impact you want to make. It can also reveal patterns in the ways you might stay stuck in your career, and what holds you back. Make notes on your reflections and any patterns you see on the map.

Your Dream Place to Work

Close your eyes and ask yourself: *Where would I love to do my ideal work?* Is it in a high-rise office? Or the ground floor of an arts center? Are you working inside? Or outside? Are you surrounded by plants or people? Or are you tucked away in an office? Imagine it. Imagine how you use the space, where you store your belongings, what your work-space looks like. Once you get an image, stay with it and study its details. Try drawing or listing some of the features of this work environment.

Internal Reflection

Imagine yourself leaving work at the end of the day at a dream job—you don't need to know what the job is yet to do this. Imagine that you are gathering your coat and bag to go home at the end of the day or shift. How do you feel as you are leaving work? What one word describes that feeling?

Then, as you go through your actual workday, note how often you get to experience that feeling. Is it hourly? Weekly? Monthly? Never? If and when you do feel it, what kind of work are you doing? These are hints about the kind of work that makes you feel alive. Ideally, your career is full of days that give you this feeling. Of course, life is life, so it isn't ideal all the time. But if you never feel how you want to feel at work, it could be time to make a change.

Spirituality

Journal about the role spirituality has in your career. Ask yourself the following questions and write down your thoughts:

- How important is it to me that my work is linked to a higher purpose?

- Does my career need to be an expression of what I feel like I was made to do?

- Do I want to bring my soul to work with me? (Sit with the answer to this one. There is no right answer.)

STEP 4 CHECK-IN

1 Were you surprised that any of your values were more or less important than you thought?

2 Did exploring your ideal work culture help you see why you have been feeling stuck in your current role?

EXPERIMENT
AND TEST

YOU NOW KNOW what your strengths are and what you value, and you have an idea of what an ideal work environment would look like to you. In a lot of traditional career coaching models, the next step would be to set a career path. But that doesn't always bring people career satisfaction.

You can't make career decisions in your head; you need to test them out with your body and your intuition. What looks great on paper may not feel good in reality. If our minds were the only thing we brought to work, that theoretical choice might turn out okay. But we don't. We bring our whole body, including our emotions and instincts. Think of how common (and unfortunate) it is to hear a person describe their work as "soul-sucking" when they aren't satisfied with their position.

The first four steps in this book asked you to do introspective work. That can be eye-opening, but it can also be debilitating because it prevents action. In this step, you will break away from thinking, and start taking that action. You have to test things in the real world, just not in your mind.

I was working with a client, Jake, who had juggled multiple jobs while being a fiction writer. He had been taking temporary, project-based positions at community and arts organizations, but when he was about to become a father he came to me. "I need to get a steady job," he said. "I'd like to get a full-time community development position where I run a program. That feels like the most lucrative option." I explained that while it seemed like an ideal role, and that he knew the sector, he still needed to test out what it would be like to have the full-time job and to be turning down writing projects. He was open to trying it.

SET THE LENGTH OF YOUR EXPERIMENT

There are a few ways to set up your experiment. Some tests can be done in a few hours, like booking an informational interview. Some, however, can take six months to two years. It can be freeing to see these career experiments as temporary—that gives you permission to try out different ideas and theories. If any don't work out, you don't have to feel like a failure, because you know you have still benefited from the learning.

Jake needed an income immediately, so he decided to test out working for an organization for at least six months. This would bring in steady income during the pregnancy, but it would also give him a decent amount of time to get to know how it felt to be in that kind of role. His career stories showed that he was great at creating things, making connections with people, and strategizing. Jake got offers for two roles, one in a set term (a nine-month maternity leave position) and one permanent and full-time. He chose to take the short-term role—a position as an environmental programs coordinator for a not-for-profit—because the project was more interesting and in line with his values.

Every week Jake reflected on how he felt at work. He wrote down what projects, accomplishments, and actions he was proud of, and rated from week to week how much he longed to write or to be working on a new novel. At the beginning of the experiment, he didn't miss writing that much, and he liked being in charge of a project. After four months had passed, he started to grow dissatisfied with the role. I asked, "Can you pinpoint what you don't enjoy?" and he said, "I like the day-to-day work, advising the team on what to do, and seeing it implemented. But I hate reporting to a board. The board meetings are long and pointless, and they feel like a waste of time. I don't enjoy creating the monthly reports, so I trained another employee to do them for me. And every week I need to submit timesheets for all the staff, and I'd rather be making things happen."

This practice helped Jake see that while he could handle the responsibility of leading a project, there were aspects of the job he avoided and found draining. Based on this experience, we talked about the work he liked most and what else it could look like. He came up with the idea of being a freelance program consultant. "Because I know how funding works at each of these places, I could advise them on how to implement the project and do the reporting," he said. "And I'd never have to deal with their boards."

While Jake was still with the not-for-profit, he started to talk to other organizations about the possibility of consulting with them on their programs. He worked with three organizations to come up with a structure and cost for his services. Once his nine-month term was up, he immediately started testing how it felt to be a consultant. He ended up loving it. Jake became a father and found a way to get steady work doing what he loved, while still being able to write novels.

Without testing, Jake might have accepted a permanent role that was not a great fit, but one that he would stay in anyway. People do this all the time. They make a career decision in their head, without knowing what it would be like in reality. Then they stay in the job longer than they should, because they believe one or more of these false ideas:

- I'll never be happy in any job.

- I made this decision, so I need to stick with it for at least three years.

- I can learn to love this job.

- I can find joy in a side project, and that will make the job feel manageable.

Experiment before committing, and you can avoid all of these traps.

Work in a Pandemic

The COVID-19 pandemic influenced almost every sector on the planet, and it changed work forever. People who believed the old storyline about secure and forever jobs found themselves without those jobs. The only thing you can rely on in your career is your story.

On the other side of that coin, the pandemic led millions to start career experiments. A videographer friend, for example, quickly scanned his list of dream projects. He moved into high gear and coordinated a weekly cooking show, where people all over the world got to cook with a professional chef. I saw freelance marketers quickly pivot and take on head of marketing roles at firms. One marketer whose job offer at a big technology company was withdrawn at the last minute quickly landed a new job with another equally cool tech company.

All of these people had different experiences, but they took a few common actions:

- They became super clear about their value and what they offer (their career brand).

- They had a list of things they dreamed about doing in their career.

- They reached out to people in their network and proposed positions and projects.

- They didn't define themselves by their job title or sector; they led with their skills.

- Once they landed a new job, they shared their story to offer hope.

If you are ever in a crunch, having stories that back up your skills is a must. When a company is in crisis, they don't have time to figure out what you are good at or how you can help them. They need people who are ready to dive in. In the pandemic, people who understood themselves and had experimented with what was out there landed in new roles quickly and happily.

We know this can happen again. It can happen if job security doesn't exist. If entire sectors can close, you're no longer building a career for safety, you're building a career to be the best expression of yourself. Be honest about what that looks like for you.

CONSIDER THE FUTURE OF WORK

When you limit yourself to acting on what you think you need next, and you never test it, you might jump into a safe role without ever trying something unfamiliar. When people think about careers, what they imagine often falls into one of four scenarios:

- The full-time job (a "job-job")
- Being self-employed
- A mix of part-time jobs that add up to a full-time job
- The full-time job + a side hustle

I have worked with people who combine the most interesting skills and jobs to make their career. I know one person, Adrian, who holds freelance roles in Canada and Italy. They spend half their year teaching part-time at a university and doing HR consulting in Canada. Then they spend the other half of the year doing bookkeeping for a family business in Italy. Before they made this their reality, Adrian had a full-time HR job. A layoff forced them to think about making a move, and they weren't sure what they wanted next. When we reviewed their career stories, we found that they loved doing work where they organized and tracked things, coached other people, and helped companies understand policies and regulations. They would be happy in any role where they got to track something, advise others, and work with HR policies. While at first glance another HR manager role made sense, their values showed they craved autonomy and needed a role where they self-led their work. That's when I had Adrian do the "ten possible selves" exercise.

Your Ten Possible Selves

I first read about the ten possible selves exercise in Herminia Ibarra's *Working Identity*. In this exercise, you write a list of eight to ten possible selves you are interested in

being. When I do this activity in my classes, the participants often simply list possible job titles, but I encourage
them to also list other possibilities they may not know the
name of yet, or attributes they'd like to highlight more, like
creativity. Adrian's list looked like this:

1   HR manager.

2   HR director with more authority to implement policies.

3   Open a vintage clothing store. I've collected vintage
    clothing for years and have an online shop that does
    well. My parents used to have a small shop and I liked
    working in it as a teenager.

4   Policy analyst (for HR, maybe government).

5   Teacher or lecturer, working with business students.

6   Open my own HR agency. I've joked about this with
    some colleagues, but I was the only one not really
    laughing. Some said they would leave to work with me
    if I started my own company.

7   People and culture leader.

8   Case studies writer (or make this more a part of my job).

9   Travel agent.

10 Bookkeeper in Italy.

On the same day that Adrian created this list they landed an interview for an HR director role, but they were going to be away in Italy at the requested interview time. They asked if they could do it over the phone instead, or possibly bump it to two weeks later. The company said they were in a rush and needed it to be soon and in person. Adrian considered canceling their trip, but I said, "I don't think you need to cancel your trip. How about you go to Italy and treat it like a career experiment. Go and relax, but also see if there is an opportunity to test out any of the jobs on your list. You never know."

Adrian turned down the interview and went to Italy for three weeks. We met a few days after their return and they said, "You know, my partner and I loved it. Their family has a business they're thinking about expanding, so I took your advice and offered to help them set up their books. I spent a week of the vacation doing that work, while my partner helped with another part of the business—they're a builder. On the flight home, I joked that maybe we could work there half of the year, you know, help the family business, and return to Canada for the other half. As we talked about it more, it became less of a joke and more of a plan. When I got home, there was a message from the university asking if I wanted to teach a human resources policy class in the fall, so this might work out."

Adrian took the university gig, connected with other people in the field to offer HR policy advice on a freelance basis, then traveled back to Italy to help with the books.

Your ten possible selves list is a starting point to begin articulating what your career could look like, and what's worth exploring.

When I ask people to make this list—especially when they're in a senior leadership role—there is often pushback. CEOs will say something like, "I'm not going to step down from being a leader. I know I want to be a CEO, just in a different company."

It's equally challenging for students, newly graduated people, or people who love their field. I often hear something like, "I didn't spend three to 15 years studying this just to start over again." It's still worth doing.

Writing down possible selves on a list doesn't mean you have to do those things. Usually people write down about three or four safe choices, job titles for things they have already done or currently do. Then they'll have two or three wild choices, like a CFO who writes "astronaut" on their list. And then usually there are one or two choices that are a complete surprise, varying from librarian to public speaker. These are the ones we're interested in. These are the selves that a person dreams of being, but has given up on. In some cases, they can remain a dream. But sometimes, people take action.

I did this exercise with my dad, whose entire career had been in railway management. He put "sportscaster" on his list. I asked him about it and he said, "I've never told anyone this, but I always thought I'd be good at doing the commentary during games." And he would have been. My dad not only understood sports, he was also incredible at connecting with people and telling stories—all the stuff a sportscaster needs to do. He never took action on this and it always remained a dream. If he had done this exercise earlier in his career, he might have acted on it. Maybe he wouldn't have become an actual sportscaster, but he might have moved into sports management or public speaking, and had more pride in his career.

Right now, list ten possible titles, sectors, or personality features you'd like to try out. Write them down here:

1 _____

2 _____

3 _____

4 _____

5 _____

6 _____

7 _____

8 _____

9 _____

10 _____

Now, take it a step further. Go back and write a bit of explanation for each possible self, and, if possible, any connections or knowledge you already have in the sector.

Look at your list. Which one are you most excited about? Are you willing to go out and test it?

I did this exercise with a client, Bertilda, who came to me because she wanted to land a corporate marketing job. On her list she wrote that she wanted to be a freelance editor. I asked her what I've asked you: "Of the ten possible selves you wrote, which is the most exciting to you?" She said, "The freelance editor role."

Then I asked, "How might you test if that could be the right move for you?" She came up with a list of people she could talk with, and what her business would look like. She went off and had those conversations, then she came back to me to say she believed she could make a go of it.

All of the skills that she needed to run her business were part of her career stories cards. She started the business, but also wrote a resume to land teaching jobs at a university—this relieved the pressure of making money right away. Now it's been two years, and her editing business is thriving.

This story is not unusual. You can combine all of your interests into one role with one company, or into several roles across multiple companies, or even countries. We're in the future of work, where transferable skills can be, and are expected to be, used in new ways. One of the best ways to explore what combination works for you is to experiment and test them out.

The idea that we are meant to be one thing, and one thing only, is ridiculous. Sometimes the work you used to love doesn't feel the same anymore. Living every day without enjoying the work you are doing can be overwhelming, especially when you don't know what comes next. This process can feel even more daunting when you're unemployed.

Instead of searching from a reactive place—that is, from looking at available jobs and trying to mold yourself into one—experiment first.

TEST A QUALITY FROM YOUR CAREER STORIES CARDS

Is there a job on the list you just made that you've dreamed about doing and that feels possible? Murphy always wanted to work in the tech industry, but her experience was in construction. We looked at the skills from her career stories cards and saw that she was great at innovation, making projects happen, and building support systems to manage that change. Murphy built a resume that highlighted those transferable skills, then heard about an open house at a new tech company that makes video games. She went to the open house and made a great first impression by asking smart questions and not pitching herself too soon. She followed up a few days later with her resume and landed a job as a product manager in technology.

How to Test Out a Career

There are many ways to experiment with different career options. Here are just a few:

- Having conversations with people in that role or sector
- Jumping in and trying it out

- Doing it as a side hustle
- Offering your services as a one-time gig
- Building a proposal
- Joining a new team or project
- Volunteering in that role or sector
- Talking about your idea with others

There are also a few ways you can assess an option to help you choose what you should experiment with:

- The easiest: the role that only requires having a conversation with someone or reading a book on the topic

- The most interesting: the role you can't forget about

- The least risky: the one that is most guaranteed or will change your life the least

- The most risky: the one that will make the biggest change for you *right now*

- The fastest: something that will result in an immediate small win, or involves the quickest action

Before you test out an idea, determine what you hope to learn and how you will assess it. Some people assess using their gut. But you'll also want to set criteria based on your values or some other measure.

It's important to remember that, at this point, you are only testing the waters. You are not committing to making a move or accepting a position. Testing offers you a new perspective, and the opportunity to grow your network. Jumping in with a permanent decision before testing could land you in the same place you are now. I prefer small wins and small lessons over big leaps.

Things change, life happens. You get to decide if you're the kind of person who is prepared to ride that change, or if you are someone who is always reacting.

Internal Career Experiments

You can absolutely do a career experiment at your current job (if you have one). This works well if you uncovered a skill you love to use but rarely *get* to use. Look for opportunities where you could practice that skill, then propose the idea to your manager. You could schedule a meeting and say something like, "I'd like to talk with you about a skill I want to develop. I'm interested in leading a team, and my current roles don't allow for that. I know you're working on a new IT project, and I'd like a seat at the table. I would bring (your specific value-add). Is that a possibility at this time?"

If a project like that isn't in the works, you could say something like, "I've been reflecting on my career and it revealed that I enjoy hiring people and I might like to move into HR in the next few years. If you hear of an opportunity to sit in on an interview panel or help select people based on their resumes, can you let me know?" Now your manager knows about your career ambitions, and can help make connections for you.

If you work for a toxic person who does not support your dreams, you might be better off doing a career experiment elsewhere. Internal career experiments are supposed to be fun, not something that makes your work life more difficult.

External Career Experiments

There are few ways to craft experiments with external companies. Sometimes it means applying for a term role and learning on the job without committing to anything longer, like Jake did. I've seen people work three days a week at their regular job and two days a week at their experimental job to get a feel for the new work.

You could also try freelancing in a new sector. This used to be only for startups, but larger corporations are becoming open to hiring freelancers to help out on special projects. If you can get insider knowledge about projects, you have an even better chance of doing an experiment (see more on this in Step 9).

Sometimes you need to keep the job you have, and the only way you can experiment is through informational interviews. These are short interviews you set up with someone who is doing the work you want to be doing. You have a conversation to find out what it's like to work at a given place, get suggestions on courses to take, or other people to call, so you can learn what the position is really like (see page 318 for examples of questions you can ask at this meeting). Some people can get invited to tour a place. Or you might just get a phone call. This process looks deceptively easy, but you may find yourself feeling resistant to taking action. We'll discuss ways to push past that resistance in Step 7.

CREATE YOUR OWN SIDE GIG

Often it's hard to land part-time or casual work in a new sector. An alternative path is to independently create your own project to learn from.

Reggie was interested in becoming a career coach but wasn't sure if it was for her. We met at a coffee shop to talk it out, and the first thing I noticed was how small she made herself in the chair. We were the same height, but the way she rolled her shoulders forward and held her head made her look teeny. She asked me how I knew I wanted to do what I do, and I explained that while I fell into it, it uses my top skills, so I found that I enjoyed it. She had read books on career coaching and had worked in HR for almost ten years. She worked in retail, creating employee handbooks, advising on compensation levels, and keeping up with employment regulations. Reggie had experience coaching employees at performance review meetings, but nothing outside of that. She thought she would love to be an independent career coach, but wasn't sure. Her career stories highlighted that she loved to make a difference, make actionable plans with people, and conduct research.

Reggie had applied for several career coaching positions, but kept being told she needed more coaching experience. (This is a common hurdle—you need experience, but no one will hire you to give you that experience.) "Just do it on your own then," I said. "Think of what you want to coach people to do, then make an offer, put it out there." Reggie said she wanted to help people with their interview skills. She had hired and interviewed people for over ten years and knew some tricks. She put together an offer and started to share it on LinkedIn and within her network.

Then, the worst thing happened. Nobody bought the interview package. Reggie modified her approach and tried again. And again, not one person replied or bought her offer.

She shared with me that she hated promoting herself and didn't like putting herself out there. I said, "That's what you're going to need to do if you're going to work for yourself. Or, you can hire someone to do the promo stuff for you. Do you enjoy working with other people to guide their work? Or do you want to learn to get over yourself so you can start to sell yourself and this product?"

Reggie said no to both. While this may seem like a failed career experiment, it wasn't. Knowing what you don't want to do is as important as knowing what you do want to do. Putting together an offer and presenting it to her network was a brave move, and it showed Reggie that a big part of being an independent coach was being able to talk about your work. She didn't like that part.

Knowing exactly what it feels like to do the work you think you want to do is one of the most critical parts of a career experiment. If you test it first, you'll know how it feels. Planning is fun and smart, but testing is where learning really happens.

Esha had the opposite experience. When I met her, I was surprised that she worked in project management because she carried herself like an artist. She seemed less interested in delivering projects on time (an absolutely necessary PM skill) and more interested in sharing ideas on how to improve things. Her career stories cards showed that she loved to be involved in improving processes, creating opportunities for others, and anything to do with innovation, so she thought she should transition from project management to working in the tech sector. Esha had never worked in tech before so she attended a few local events, and after a few months she became close with a group of women. In listening to them, she saw that they experienced some barriers to success and opportunity, so she asked if they wanted to start a Women in Tech group to raise awareness about their skills and inspire others to get involved in tech. They made it happen, and she worked with the group to put on events. In her career experiment she got close with a senior-level woman, who ended up offering Esha a management job at her tech firm.

If it's possible for you to build a small-scale project to see if you like doing it, do so. The benefit of this type of career experiment is that you can use it as experience. It becomes another story you can share about your career. Even if you fail, that story of failure could be the exact one to help you land an ideal job.

KNOW YOUR CAREER HEROES

For some, the idea of making a list of titles is uninspiring. It holds them back more than brings out possibilities. Others say they can't make the list because they don't even know what job title the skills from their career stories cards fall under. The career heroes exercise is another way to find out what you should be experimenting with.

Career heroes are people who you admire. The ones you think have figured out what they're doing with their work life. They might even be people you are envious of. I use this exercise often when I'm teaching job-searching to professionals who have returned to school after working for many years. "Write out a list of people who you think have it made," I tell them. "Who has a career that you think is awesome? Who would you love to switch places with for a day or for a year?" It might be people you know, I say, or even people in your family. It might be someone famous. Then I give them time to make their lists, and I tell them not to hold back.

When they're done, I have them review their lists. "What do the people on your list do?" I ask. "In what way do they carry themselves that you admire?" I ask my students to analyze their work and actions the same way they did with their career stories. What story does this person model by how they show up and what they do?

From there, I ask my students to narrow down their list and share the common skills they see in their career heroes. They don't have to name names, just the skills they admire. One student, Ash, said, "Every career hero of mine paved their own way. They're self-made; they saw a problem, and then worked to fix it." I asked, "Have you done that too?" He nodded. "Yeah," he said. "In some ways I have, but mostly on a personal level." I said, "Maybe your next step is to look for a problem you could solve. Then you can test how it feels to work that way, and if you want to do that your whole career."

Another student cut in. "I have lots of problems I'd love for you to help with," they said. We all laughed. I encouraged each student to compare the features of their career heroes and see if they could try to emulate those coveted skills in their own life—especially when it matched up with skills they discovered through their career stories cards.

I gave them a few weeks to experiment and bring back their findings. One day, Ash came into class looking like a changed person, and I asked him what happened.

"I was searching for a way to help and pave my own way," he said. "I gave family and friends advice about budgeting and time management, but it didn't feel like a real experiment or test. That's just how I am. But then, two days ago, we had a big dispute at work. A large order came in and wasn't input into the system properly. That meant a bunch of us needed to stay late and fulfill the order. This was the third time it happened, and management was mad because they have to pay overtime. In fact, we were all mad because we're part-time for a reason."

Ash told me how he went up to his supervisor and asked if he could look at the way the data was input into the program. "At first he laughed," he said. "I'm just a floor worker. But I told him that I'm studying programming at university, and that I might be able to help." The supervisor got one of the admins to show Ash the program, and walked him through how to enter information. "As he showed me the process, I saw where he could add one step that would ensure all orders were shared with my team," he said. "I spoke to management to get their approval to implement this step and they agreed. It's only been a few days, but the new process is working and I don't think the error will happen again. My manager was impressed with me, and asked me to remind him when I fully graduate. He said there could be more work for me."

I almost cried when I heard this. All Ash did was try on an attribute of one of his career heroes, and by doing so he changed the trajectory of his career. This experiment allowed him to add another skill to his career stories, and get even clearer on his eventual career target.

If you don't get clarity through your career experiments, keep testing until you feel ready to pick a position and land it. Experiments are inherently risky—they require you to stop thinking about something and actually try it out. Some lifelong dreams might get crushed, but you will get closer to knowing what your next move will look like. And what's even more important is how you'll feel when you have the career you want.

ACTIVITIES TO SUPPORT STEP 5

Ten Possible Selves

If you haven't already done so, write out your "ten possible selves" list (see page 103). One you have your list, arrange them in a chart using one of the following orders:

- The easiest
- The most interesting
- The least risky
- The most risky
- The fastest

Estimate how long your career experiment will take, and plan out how you will do it. Then, take action and assess the results.

Career Stories Review

Every day, morning and night, take out your career stories cards, get still, and read your top three career skills again. Practice saying, *I am great at (skill 1), (skill 2), and (skill 3)*. These are the foundation of your career brand no matter what work you'll do. Know them; model them.

Change Plan

Make a list of changes that would improve your current situation. Be sure to include habits or activities that don't add value or energy to your day-to-day. They might be small changes ("stop looking at my phone upon waking"; "wash the car") or big ones ("start running again"; "stop letting Frank take credit for my work"). To increase their "sticky factor," make them specific and time-bound, like so:

- I resolve to run every Monday.
- I resolve to do laundry every Wednesday.
- I resolve to not use my phone for one 24-period every two weeks.

Career Heroes

If you haven't done so yet, do the career heroes exercise. Think about people who you have great respect and admiration for. People who you feel have figured out their career. What have they done? What could you start to do that have that feeling for yourself? What action could you take this week that is like your career hero? Try it for a week and see how it feels. Does it help you feel any closer to knowing what kind of work you could do?

Dream Job Search

Go back to your ideal job description from Step 4. Type the keywords and features into a job search site and see if any positions come up. Or, call up three people in your network and describe your dream job to them. Ask if they know of anything like the position you're describing.

STEP 5 CHECK-IN

1   What did you do as your career experiment? What did you learn? Did you gather enough information to move to the next step?

2   Did you do any activities this month to support self-connection? What were they and how did they feel? If you didn't show yourself a kindness one day this month, why not?

3   Did any other issues come up for you that stopped you from doing a career experiment? If so, what are they?

SET AND RESEARCH YOUR IDEAL WORK TARGET

ONCE YOU'VE DONE your career experiments, the next step is to choose your target. A target is where you are aiming to go. It might be a feeling, it might be a job title. Some people call it their north star. It's the thing you're moving toward.

Every great marketer knows they need to identify their audience before they can start building their campaigns. It's the same in job search. If you try to be everything for everyone, you'll end up being ignored and getting lost. Having a target ensures that the next actions you take are intentional, meaningful, and help you get what you want.

You need a target if you want your job search to be successful. A target makes it clear what kind of job you're looking for, in what sector or environment, and how you will contribute to it. But to be effective, your target has to be well chosen and specific. Here are some examples of lazy targets:

- "I will take anything in communications."

- "I can do all kinds of work. I'll even do entry-level to get my foot in the door."

- "I want to work in a big organization where I can grow."

These targets are lazy because they lack specificity and they sound desperate. They are focused on you as the job seeker, instead of what you can do for your employer. Detail is the key to making a target more clearly defined. Look what happens when you add detail to the lazy targets you just read:

- "I am looking for a small communications company where I can assist people with managing their files and projects."

- "I'm best at collecting and sorting data to help companies improve their services. I enjoy being the middle person between executives and other data scientists."

- "I'm looking for an HR role where I get to hire and onboard employees within a large, multi-site organization. I set people at ease, and have trained over 1,000 people in the electronics sector."

Some people worry that a precise target will stop them from getting offers. I've never seen that happen. What I have seen is people being recognized for being ultra-specific about their targets and having other jobs proposed to them. Why? People who have their stuff together and know what they want are far more attractive than people who seem desperate or confused.

Advertising that you are open for anything makes you look uncertain. A potential employer might think, "They don't actually know what makes them happy or what they want to do. This could be an expensive hire."

If you're constantly changing what you're good at and what you offer, people will doubt your expertise. I knew one independent coach who marketed herself as "helping companies tell their stories" when I met her. We exchanged a few messages on LinkedIn and then I stopped noticing her. A few months later, I was surprised to see that she was selling herself as a life coach for high achievers. A few months after that, she simply said she was a life coach.

When people look to hire independent practitioners, there is a long selling curve. I hired my first marketing coach after following her for three years. If she had rebranded herself three times in three years, I would have questioned her expertise. She did slightly adapt her branding now and then, but her consistency had me willing to pay top dollar to work with her.

A target gives you clarity and guides the rest of the process. If you take the time to review your career stories and values and conduct meaningful career experiments, choosing a target will be easier and less terrifying.

Give this process the time it needs. Trust your skills. Trust your stories. Think about the career experiments you did in Step 5, and answer the following questions:

What were you surprised to learn about?

_____

_____

Which of your possible selves was different than you expected?

_____

_____

Which did you find the most exciting to talk about and explore?

_____

_____

Which feels most in line with your values and the skills from your career stories cards?

_____

_____

There are different kinds of targets, and any target is good as long as it helps you understand what you're trying to achieve. Let's go over the four most common types of targets: growth targets, job targets, sector targets, and activity targets.

SET YOUR GROWTH TARGETS

Growth targets are for when you decide you want to develop a specific set of skills or build up your experiences. These types of goals help you professionally, and often don't require you to change jobs or sectors. You can work on these skills within your existing job. Not every career goal is about finding new work.

Darnell was taking HR courses on a part-time basis while working full-time at an insurance company. You could tell by how he held himself that he could reach any goal he set. He was in his early 30s, and he wanted to stop being a yes person. His five-year goal was to land an HR position and build incredible teams. But he knew he needed to develop more skills to even qualify for those jobs.

Darnell reviewed a current HR job posting and looked at the job requirements. He noted which skills he had and which ones he didn't have yet. Almost every job asked for experience leading teams and interviewing people. He had never done that. Darnell set that as his growth target, outlined how he would achieve that target, and set a timeline. His plan went like this:

- I will gain experience leading teams in the next six months by talking to my manager about involving me in a larger project.

- I will gain experience interviewing others in the next year by volunteering at a not-for-profit where they need a board member to be present at interviews.

This gave Darnell a clear plan on what to do next. He scheduled a conversation with his manager and shared that he was interested in leading a team on something. He said that if a project came up over the next three months, he would like the opportunity to lead a team. There were no existing projects at the time, but after a month, his manager approached him about a small environmental pilot program they wanted to launch. He was invited to co-lead the project and the team.

At the same time, Darnell reached out to a community volunteer organization and asked if there were any roles that would allow him to interview others. The person who answered said, "That's exactly the help we're looking for here." He took on the role, planning and leading a few interviews a month.

Does this look and sound like a career experiment? It is. The difference here is that you typically do career experiments to find out if something is right for you. Taking action on a growth target, however, is something you do when you know what you want next. Figuring out your career is tricky, and Darnell might have learned that he didn't like interviewing people. If that happened, he could reflect, adapt, and set a new target.

A growth target works when you are happy in your job, but you want to improve how you show up. I had another client, Dylan, who realized through doing career experiments that he was happy in his role and company, and expected to stay there for at least three years. But he still often made small errors that earned his boss's distrust, and he feared he might be let go. Dylan's growth target went like this:

- I will learn to focus better by mapping out my time and double-checking my work. I will have zero errors in one month's time.

Dylan started to change the way he showed up at work, and just as planned, in one month's time, he had met his target. He started looking for other small targets he could reach on the way to becoming the kind of worker he would be proud to be.

Don't worry about making the wrong choice. You can always choose a new growth target to enrich your career.

SET YOUR JOB TARGETS

Some people know they need to leave their existing job—or even sector—to find ideal work. If this is you, the career experiments in Step 5 helped you see where you should be looking. The clearer you are on a target, the better. Knowing the specific title isn't enough; you also need to know your ideal targets for each aspect of the job:

- Culture
- Salary range
- Clients and co-workers
- Tasks

Be as clear as you can about the title and company you're aiming for. The clearer you can get on these things, the easier the next steps will become. Ideally, if someone were to ask you, "Hey, what's your dream job?" you could give a clear answer that showed you had thought of every detail. That doesn't mean you'll automatically land that job, but it does mean you'll have clarity about your career dreams. That clarity will give you something to work with, so you can make decisions about your next steps.

SET YOUR SECTOR TARGETS

In some cases, people don't have a specific job target. They just know they want to work in a certain sector.

There can be danger in basing your career on a sector. Sometimes, you start with a focus on the sector you love, but over time, you learn that you could do that work anywhere. If you've always worked in the same sector, test using your favorite skills outside of that sector. If it feels good, you might want to set your target as a specific job, or something in a new sector, rather than staying in the same place.

At the same time, if you've always worked in, say, publishing—you know publishing and you love it—you can choose to stay in the same sector, but in a different role. If the only clarity you have right now is the sector, that can be enough to run with. Your career brand can become "I am great at (skill 1 from your career stories cards), (skill 2), and (skill 3) and I'm looking to work in (name of sector)."

SET YOUR ACTIVITY TARGETS

If you're not looking to change jobs, develop skills, or change sectors, but you still want to grow your career, you'll likely have an activity target. An activity target is a single project you'll commit to doing. Examples of common activity targets could be:

- Starting a podcast
- Writing articles on LinkedIn
- Proposing a new department at your company
- Writing a book
- Starting your own side hustle
- Moving your side hustle to a full-time company
- Starting a not-for-profit or charity

All of these can be career builders and bring career joy. If you're planning an independent project, you'll want to be clear about why you're doing it, what will change in your life from having done it, and why you're the right person to do this project right now.

Peta was a VP in a not-for-profit. Her career stories showed she was incredible at building and leading change, operations management, and storytelling. She had helped the not-for-profit she worked for grow from ten employees to over 70. She helped propose the changes, led all of the change management processes, and built new departments from scratch. When Peta came to me, she was feeling unsure about what to do next. She got paid well and used her favorite skills at work, but she felt she had outgrown the company.

Peta was involved in a local storytelling group and her career experiment was about leading a program outside of her company. She ran a pilot program and found it freeing to build outside the restraints of a company. Her new target became laying the foundation for her own consulting business.

I asked her, "Why are you doing this? How will this change your life and why are you the right person to have a consulting firm?" She said, "I'm doing this because building is what I do best. Starting my own company will allow me to guide and inform change at a wider scale, and ensure that change helps companies, and makes them sustainable. It will change my life because instead of being overwhelmed by leading my own team through constant change, I can help others lead instead. I will have more energy for my storytelling projects. I am the right person to do this right now because I have done this for 20 years. In my research, I haven't found any other freelance consultant who has a PhD in operations management and who still wants to work alongside people through change. My career stories show me that, time after time, I need to use the exact skills the new business will need."

Powerful.

If your career testing showed you that it's time to take action on your career, starting a business could be the right next move for you. Do the activities at the end of this step to become ultra-clear about why *this* time is right, and why *this* target is the next natural step for your career story.

SET A DEADLINE

Set a date for meeting your target—specifically, when you want to actually be doing the new work.

To do this, you need to set two deadlines: your "want to work" date and your "need to work" date. Your "want to work" date is the day that, ideally, you will be working in this new job. Your "need to work" date is when your unemployment or low salary will start to negatively affect your financial situation—like having difficulty with your mortgage payments, or eating into your savings.

Define both of those dates.

These parameters build in a safety net for you. Say you know you have enough money or energy to do your current job for one more year. In this case, you might set your "want to work" date for four months, and your "need to work" date for one year. If you don't land your ideal job in four months, come back to your plan and adjust it, for example, being less selective about the location. This gives you a clear road map, and permission to go for your dream without losing anything.

You might choose to set a target a few weeks from now, or a few years. As you implement your plan, you can adjust the dates and actions to match reality.

Remember: your target is not separate from your career brand—it is a part of it. You chose it based on your career stories, experiences, and testing. Everything you have done in your career and as part of the Career Stories Method leads you to this one consistent brand.

Your career brand now looks like this:

I work best when I am (skill 1), (skill 2), and (skill 3).
I want to bring these skills to (enter target).

CONDUCT YOUR RESEARCH

Once you have a target, you want to know it like no other. Everything moving forward is going to be about how your career stories help your target. That is the foundation of your career brand. This will prevent you from becoming a career chameleon, someone who changes their focus, language, and skills depending on what is available. Instead, you'll be speaking the language of your target role so well, it's like you already work there.

Industry Terminology

The first thing you need to do is learn to talk the talk. Put yourself in a good position to land a job by using phrases and keywords in your resume, marketing materials, and interview answers that are specific to the industry.

Every industry has their own particular terminology. If you're switching industries, the sooner you can start talking like your target audience the better. Sometimes the nuances are subtle. For example, if you spent most of your career working in the retail sector, you're probably used to calling the people who buy stuff "customers." If you want to land a job in the insurance field, where they call people "clients," you'll want to change your language from customers to clients. Every time you use a phrase or term that the industry doesn't use, you look less and less like a great fit.

It works the same for starting a business or side hustle. You need to know what words and language are important for your client, so that your messaging connects with them in the right way. Weave the words you are comfortable with into your repertoire. You never want to sound like a robot—this strategy works best when you mix traditional sector words with your own vocabulary. It gives you an instant voice.

Luckily, getting access to all a sector's secret words is easy. Simply find an industry association or an industry magazine, and look up the websites of a few companies. Read through their material and make note of any words that keep getting repeated. Then, make the following lists.

Technical Words: Processes, theories, or programs, often related to skills you get training in.

- Accounting
- Algorithm
- Analysis
- Benchmarking
- Budget planning
- Change management

- Content management system (CMS)
- Customer support
- Database management
- Debugging
- Delegation
- Design
- Documentation
- Modeling
- Performance review
- Project planning
- Research
- Scheduling
- Search engine optimization (SEO)
- Software (this will be specific)
- Technical writing

Business Words: Terms that leaders and executives use to describe their work—these will often be less technical, and they will change depending on the sector. The six terms in the right-hand column in the list that follows, for example, are from a quick LinkedIn search on the language used by banking executives.

- Accountability
- Boosting morale
- Motivator
- Natural leader
- Precision
- Problem solving
- Teamwork

- Advisement
- Best-in-class
- Business acumen
- Entrepreneurial mindset
- Execution
- Repositioning

Soft and Slang Words: Words people in the industry or within a particular company use refer to and speak with each other in casual conversation. (At an IT company I once worked with, for example, the programmers called everyone who works in the admin side "suits" and themselves "hoods" because they wore hoodies.) These can be harder to find, but you might notice them in places like Reddit or Twitter, or on blogs written by industry insiders.

- Alignment
- Awesome
- Blazers
- Builder
- Forward-looking
- Growth mindset
- Hustle
- Intentional
- Play hard, work hard
- Suits
- Switcharoo
- Synergy
- Techies
- Thrive
- Tremendous
- Wizards

Entrepreneurial Words: The more you use the language of your ideal client and connect it to your career brand, the easier it is for that client to see how you can help them.

Your target clients have likely voiced these words as they discussed their problems online—a great place to look is Quora or Twitter. If they say "I feel stuck" instead of "I feel stalled," follow that lead. By incorporating the words of the client or sector, you secure your place as an expert.

- I need guidance...
- I'm overwhelmed by...
- I need clarity and direction about...
- It feels like my soul is being sucked out...

Business Acumen

If you want to get promoted at your current job, the best thing you can learn is business acumen. Go beyond using the company and industry words and figure out how your company makes money. Learn how each department functions and how money flows in and out of the company.

How do the skills from your career stories cards help the company make more money or improve how it operates?

When you have encounters with upper management, even if it's just in meetings, you want to be heard speaking with business acumen. When you suggest ideas or share updates, link your ideas and projects with the overall company. One way to remain stuck in the same role indefinitely is to only speak about how things are going in your current role and department. Linda, who was a midwife, wanted to move into management in the health sector. She researched how the department was funded and what management issues existed. At staff meetings Linda shared stories about an administrative process she tried improving. She suggested new ways of managing client intake and follow-up instead of telling individual birth stories. Leadership noticed this change and asked her to be on policy and advisory panels. This experience led her to be qualified for a leadership role within a few years. The process of changing how the leadership teams sees you starts with the stories and suggestions you share.

Industry Struggles

As you're looking for keywords, also note any topics that keep repeating. This will give you insight into some common industry struggles or issues.

Edie, who previously worked as a teacher, was applying to work at a not-for-profit arts center as a community programs manager. In her research, she often read about how arts programs struggled to be financially secure. In her work as a teacher, she had once proposed an arts program, and got significant private funding to run it. When she went into the job interview, she replied to all the specific questions they asked her, but also found opportunities to bring up her experience as a fundraiser. This caught the attention of the hiring committee, especially the board, and she was offered the job.

It doesn't always come this easily, but see if you can find any overarching problems the industry is currently facing. Then, find ways to show how you can solve those problems.

Social Media

One of the ways we can understand a company or sector is to listen to what they're talking about. If you know people who work in your target organization, you probably already know this. If you don't, you can start to learn by looking at their social media, and following current employees on LinkedIn and Twitter to see what they talk about there. Following industry-specific media and magazines is also a good idea.

Don't forget about the main social media feeds of the company you want to work for. Spend 30 minutes reading through their Twitter, Facebook, and Instagram feeds, gathering information about what your target company is hoping to do.

- Make notes on the story they explicitly tell the public about their work and purpose.

- Make notes about the story they are more subtly telling by how they interact with their stakeholders and clients.

- Make notes on what terms you keep seeing them use, including technical, business, and slang words.

If you're an entrepreneur, check out what your ideal clients talk about and share. Are they following luxury brands and dreaming about making a lot of money? Or are they following zero-waste and capsule wardrobe accounts? What story are they telling by what they follow?

Individuals

If you're looking to directly contact individual people for collaborations, research what kinds of collaborations or projects that person has done before. But don't forget: no one really cares about you. Harsh, I know. But it's true.

Before you reach out, ask yourself four questions:

- What is this person telling themselves about what work is important to them?

- Are they already collaborating with someone on a similar project?

- What do I want from this person? Advice, collaboration, an introduction?

- What could I do for or say to this person that would help them further the story they care about?

While our career brand is incredibly interesting to us, other people have to know why it might be interesting for them too. The easiest way to get there is through examining their own brand and stories.

Job Ads

If you're looking to land a new job, find a few postings for positions you would like to have. Go through them and look for common phrases, qualifications, and specific skills. Jot those down. Ensure you have the skills they are asking for, and the career stories to back them up.

Your stories do not need to be from your target industry. If you worked in manufacturing as a CNC operator and you're applying to work at a bakery as a logistics manager, you're still bringing skills with you. Say the bakery job is asking that all applicants have experience packing boxes. Maybe you've never packed a box, but you can determine that the underlying skill they need is someone who follows orders. Now, you can tell a specific story about a time you followed directions.

The Competition

If you're an entrepreneur, look at what your competition is offering and what needs they address. Look at their offers, or even buy what they're selling to experience what it's like to be their client. Think about how your offer would be different. What would make it even more valuable? How could you help people more? If a client is being served well with their program, could you offer a service that begins before or after what they do? Don't be scared off if there are a lot of people offering something similar—that often means there is demand for that service. Your work is to figure out what story the competition is sharing and how yours differs.

ACTIVITIES TO SUPPORT STEP 6

Understanding Yourself

Get clear on what you want. Journal on the following questions:

- What kind of work do I want to do?

- How do I want to help?

- What kind of results will I bring to the organization?

- What kind of work environment supports my work style and personality?

- How do I work differently from other people in my field?

Skills Strategy

Name the target and find the skills gaps. If it's a specific job, look at some available job postings and see if you would qualify for the job right now. If yes, move onto the next steps. If no, write out the skills that you need more experience in. Then, write out your target clearly: "I will develop (insert skill) by (say how you'll do it) by (give yourself a deadline)." Do this for every skill you want to develop.

Affirmation

Write down your target job as an affirmative statement. Use this format: "I will land a job as a (enter the title) for a company that is (name the company or the company values, size, culture, etc.)." For a specific job, it might look like this:

- "I will land a job as a writer for a new independent TV show that values collaboration."

- "I will land a job as a hairstylist at the Easy Cuts Salon."

- "I will be the number one wealth advisement coach in New York City."

- "I will be the next independent floral designer to win an award."

Write out this statement ten times every morning and every night.

Practice

Say your career target out loud, often. I like to do this in the mirror. Combine your career stories skills with your target: "Hello, I'm Kerri Twigg and I work to help people, solve problems, and build programs that double the revenue of any organization. I am going to create a career coaching program that changes how people talk about work." Do this every day.

Date Setting

If you haven't done so yet, write out your "need to work" and "want to work" dates. Be realistic about both of them. Once you have your dates, write out what actions you'll take every week, month, or year until you reach the target. Allocate time in your schedule to do the work. How will you assess if you met these goals or not?

Research

Read articles and reports from your target sector. What words are being used by industry professionals? How might you adapt the wording of your skills to match this?

- Can you see what problems people in your target industry struggle to solve? How do the three skills from your career stories cards place you to solve that problem? Try practicing making that case aloud.

- Find some sample job ads and look for qualifications they care about and what words they're using in their ad.

- Research and take a class with someone who is already doing your ideal work. Make notes on how you could make it better and even more valuable for people.

STEP 6 CHECK-IN

1   How do you feel now that you have a target?

2   Did any other issues come up that stopped you from committing to a target? If so, what are they?

3   What are the most surprising words that your target uses? Are there one or two words you could start using alongside your regular vocabulary?

4   Is there a problem that you can solve for your target? Have you practiced telling it?

5   Did your research make it even clearer that you chose the right target? If not, what came up and how can you test it before moving into marketing yourself for this target? What do you need to check out first?

TEND TO YOUR CAREER MINDSET

THE REST OF the Career Stories Method is going to ask you to take action, believe in your dreams, trust your value, and start putting yourself out there like you never have before. That doesn't come easily for anyone. It's one thing to experiment a little and set a date, and another thing to actually take action on your dreams. It's time to examine your mindset about work.

Here's what I know about you:

- You are worthy of doing work you love.

- You are awesome.

- You have a particular set of skills and experiences that make you an incredible asset.

- You can have career success and feel incredible at work.

- You can trust you are enough.

I've never met anyone who didn't deserve meaningful work. The big question is, what's holding you back from going for ideal work?

When I ask people this, these are the reasons I most commonly hear:

- Fear
- Lack of security
- Not wanting to start over
- Invested too much time or energy in another field
- Too much work or education to make it happen
- Not the right time

It's easy to doubt ourselves, doubt our values, and doubt that we will ever land ideal work. Sometimes, we find out halfway through our plan that we weren't being honest with ourselves about the kind of work we actually want to do. Pay attention to everything you feel about this in your process of discovery.

There are the practical aspects of finding new work, like writing a resume or figuring out what you actually want to do. The other side is taking care of yourself during this process. A common mistake is to believe that, once you know your target and have the marketing pieces in place, you'll land ideal work. I wish that were true. To be honest, the hardest part is when you're taking all the right steps and you still haven't landed ideal work.

Going for your career dreams can run you ragged because the process is full of self-questioning, stretch activities, rejections, and refining. I have seen people push so hard to reach their career dreams that they burn out; they are in no physical or mental state to start new work.

DEAL WITH REJECTION

After you know your career stories and you are actively getting out there and putting in the work, the biggest struggle is getting through the transition, especially the rejection part. It's normal to be amazing and still not make headway on landing ideal work right away.

Think back to Anton, the graphic designer turned videographer. He hit a small bump as he took action toward his career dreams. Anton decided he would start making videos again, and ordered a $2,000 camera online—a huge purchase for him. He also bought a camera cage, batteries, a new lens, and other parts. When the camera arrived, he eagerly opened the package and turned it on. It worked for a second, then it died. He tried again. It kept happening. Anton had to return the camera and argue with the seller about paying a restocking fee. We had a call and he said, "This transaction set me back a month. Do you think it's a sign that I'm not supposed to do this work?"

I agreed that it sounded frustrating. I said, "That's a lot of money if you've never spent money on your dream before. And it sounds like you were excited to take action on your career, and now it's a month later and nothing is different. The first thing we can do is look at your target dates. Do you need to adjust anything there?"

When he looked at his scheduled career transition plan, he realized he wasn't behind at all. He had mapped out three months to get a camera and do tests. That made him feel better. Reality-check any setbacks you experience: it's likely you're further ahead than you give yourself credit for.

Frustration is an emotion that can have a physical component that many can actually learn to locate in their body. Doing this work can reduce the amount of power that frustration has in your life. I encouraged Anton to do a body scan to deal with his frustration.

You Can Handle This

Going for your dreams is harder than it looks. Along with the actual work of preparing your resume, networking, and making interview notes is the emotional work. You start to dream about how your life is going to be once you have ideal work. You might even plan what bus route you'll take, how you'll cancel your gym membership and work out on campus, and what you'll wear. So when you experience setbacks from getting work you are qualified for, it hurts.

Some people will advise you to protect yourself by not getting your hopes up about a role. I've never been able to do this. I cared about every role I applied to. I've also seen people decide to play it cool in their job search—what happens is that they end up sending the message that they don't care if they land the job or not. That's not enticing for the hiring company.

You have recovered from rejection before. You can do it again. And know that any time you start to feel you're pushing too hard, look at your schedule and block off some self-connection time.

CONTEXTUALIZE YOUR REJECTION

Comparison is a great tool for putting rejection into an acceptable context. On the first day of an oral communications class that I teach at university, I always ask my students to write down on paper what they are most scared of about the class. I collect the notes and read them aloud. Most say "getting up in front of everyone." Taking action on your career and sharing stories is very much like getting up in front of everyone. To ease their worries I teach this comparison method, to help them put things into perspective.

First, I instruct the class to think of the greatest loss of their life. For some, it may be the loss of a parent, a child, a friend. For others it may be the loss of a marriage or a job or their home. We have all lost something.

Next, I say, "Okay. If you're comfortable, we're going to lean into that loss. We're going to take some time to tune in to the feeling of that loss." If the loss they first thought of is too strong for this moment, I tell them to choose a slightly less terrible loss. "Now," I say, "when you experienced that loss, where did you feel it in your body? See if you can conjure up some of the feeling again. Pay attention to it and watch how the feeling dissipates the more you do so. Now, think about getting up in front of the class and giving a talk about something that you prepared. Where do you feel that feeling in your body? Is it as heavy?"

Every time, there is laughter. They laugh because the fear of standing up in front of their class is so much smaller than the great loss they have already experienced in their life.

"Replay in your mind's eye how you got over the loss," I say next. "Try to re-create in your imagination the steps you took to get over the loss. Acknowledge the happy times beyond that loss that you survived. Witness and acknowledge that you have survived loss before and can do it again. Trust you have all the skills—because you do—to cope with this new challenge of getting up in front of the class."

There is more laughter. Using this method doesn't mean they won't still feel nervous on presentation day. But it does mean that they'll know they can get through it.

You can too. You have already been through worse. And, yes, absolutely, it takes huge guts to take action on your dreams. But the alternative is harder. The alternative is to stay in an average type of career, and we both know that you have more to share than that. You've got this. Really.

LET GO OF "LIKE"

Hey, it's okay if they don't like you! One of the biggest lessons of my life is accepting that I'm not going to be liked by everyone. The problem is that I really like to be liked. I enjoy being liked so much that I would adapt my personality and sacrifice my well-being and values to try to please others. Often, that didn't even work.

Francine shared that her manager was awful to her. No matter what she tried, she could not get this manager on her side. She came to me to see if there was anything she could do, a story she could tell, that could get her manager to like her. I said, "Nope, I don't know how to teach you that. I am interested though . . . what do you respect about your manager?"

Francine laughed and said, "Not much."

She told me she was thinking about leaving the company. Instead of trying to make her manager like her, Francine got clear on the kind of people she wanted to work with in her next role. She ended up landing a job quickly through her network. I saw her a few months later and she laughed about her old manager. She said, "I can't believe I cared so much about what she thought about me back then. You know, after I quit, things started to fall apart over there and my old manager called me to say that she was sorry for how she treated me. It was like once I stopped trying so hard, she could really see me."

This happens. Not always, but this happens.

It's difficult for people pleasers—like me—to accept that it's okay to not be liked. There are things I don't like. I can see why other people like them, they're just not for me. Many others are like that too.

I've been lucky in my business in that I haven't struggled to land clients. At one point I had taken on too many, so I started to pay attention to which ones were draining to work with and which ones energized me. I noticed a few common characteristics and thought, "Okay, if I don't want to work with this type of client, how do I show I am not right for them? That they should work with another type of coach?" Then I started to intentionally talk about my work and process in a way that that type of person wouldn't like.

I started to attract even more of my type of person. I started to have less stress, while showing what was unique about me.

Things feel better when you're working with the right people. You'll have a better chance of a thriving career if you're selective about who you work with. You probably want to work with people who understand and bring out the best in you, right? That means modeling and sharing stories in a way that gets those people's attention. Everyone else can find and hire someone who would be a better fit.

It's okay to not be liked. It's good business.

DON'T BE AFRAID OF FEAR

Fear is a wild experience. I don't think anything holds people back more in their career than fear. Fears can range from practical things, like not making enough money, to negative self-beliefs, like "I'm not the kind of person who gets to love their work. Who do I think I am?"

Here's what I know about that. I think you can feel and have fear and then do it anyway. It's not about denying that fear exists, it's about denying the power it has over your career. I have never met anyone who was not worthy of having awesome work, no matter how they defined it. The more you devote yourself to work that brings you deep fulfillment, the more fear dissipates.

I'm not a big fan of "fake it till you make it" but I am a big believer in "feel it and do it anyway." For many years I didn't take action on my career dreams. I told myself that I wasn't the type of person who got to do amazing work, and then I did it anyway. I followed all of the steps I share in this book, and it changed my life in many ways—and gave me a career I love.

The only way it worked, though, was through a combination of examining my stories and taking action.

ACTIVITIES TO SUPPORT STEP 7

Coping with Setbacks

Deal with rejections and setbacks as they happen. Your journey to getting what you want in your career is not going to be straight and easy just because you know your career brand. As each rejection or setback happens, put it into perspective, deal with it, and keep on going. You've got this.

Career Dream Enemies

Make a list of your career dream enemies. These are people from your past who made things difficult for you or teased you when you tried to take action on your dreams. Be specific about who stopped you, and what they did. This list may grow as you go through this process. These enemies might be from your childhood—someone who made fun of you for raising your hand or saying the wrong answer at school. You don't need to carry them or their discouragement with you anymore. Once you have a few names, burn the list or counter the name with a positive affirmation. Then repeat.

Expressing Your Intention

Share that you're thinking about a career move with a few friends. As they react and share their opinions, whether negative or positive, practice letting their reaction happen without any need to explain or defend.

Career Obituary

This one might seem a bit morbid, but it works. Write out your own career obituary. Imagine yourself at the end of your career, looking back, then map out where you went from this present moment. Did you go for the dream? What happened? This exercise is amazingly effective because it helps you to see how short life is—why waste it doing work you hate? Try writing your first draft out here:

_____

_____

_____

_____

_____

_____

_____

_____

_____

STEP 7 CHECK-IN

1   Did you do any activities this month to support self-connection? What were they and how did they feel? If you didn't show yourself a kindness one day this month, why not?

2   Did any other issues come up for you that challenged you to stop believing in yourself or your worth? If so, what are they? What did you do to deal with those feelings?

—

BECOME A BETTER STORYTELLER

—

T HE FINAL STEPS of the Career Stories Method ask you to start sharing your work with other people, and the best way to do that is through the stories you tell. Stories have an incredible way of helping people understand you and the work you've done. You're here to build an extraordinary career, and your stories share that.

You have three types of stories to focus on and develop as you nurture your career:

Your Career Brand: You've already been building this one. It's the story about the three skills you're good at and what ideal work is for you. It comes from the skills from your career stories cards, combined with your values and target. Often this story is the same for a few years. It might change when you land a new job, complete a project, or discover you get pleasure from using another skill.

The Story Your Target Is Telling Themselves: It doesn't matter if you're looking to land a job-job, love your current job more, or run your own business and find clients. You are serving a target and they have an idea about themselves. Any time you tell a story that contradicts their core story, they're likely going to get angry or step away. For example, if an investment company tells themselves a story about being relevant to people in their 20s, and you write an article about how investing starts in your 40s, you're telling different stories.

The Stories You Tell: These are the stories you tell in the way you carry your body, show up in person and online, create content, and speak with people.

The first four steps built your core story. The sixth step defined your target's story. And the seventh step got you ready to handle anything that comes up for you. Now, we'll focus on how to become a better storyteller.

RELEASE YOUR INNATE STORYTELLER

Storytelling is a human gift. Our brains love to hear stories and are wired to understand them. People don't want to hear information, especially when they're thinking about working with you. They want to know where you've been, what difference you've made, and what you want to do next. They want to have faith in your work and in you.

Sadly, that message hasn't reached all of us. Many of us were told the best way to grow our career is to not complain, to show up, to let our work ethic be our best advertising feature, and to "say the right things" at the interview. It can be hard to recognize that you need to develop story skills. "Stories" may sound too childish for some and too creative for others, but stories are the secret to career growth.

You might have been told that talking about your work is bad. At some point in the past you either saw someone being judged for celebrating their own work, or you were personally shamed. But knowing what makes you awesome and sharing that with other people is not bad.

You are not full of yourself. You are not saying you're more valuable than any other human on this planet. You're actually doing people a favor by sharing what you're awesome at and providing solid examples that help them see how incredible you are. Then they can know you're the right one to hire.

When you hide or are coy about your career brand, your career stories, and your skills, you won't get chosen. Someone else who tells a better story will get selected.

So start telling incredible and memorable stories. It'll change your life. Here's how.

BE ALERT TO YOUR BODY POSTURE

Your body is a huge part of your career story. If you're looking to land new work, you need to be aware of what your body is doing as you tell your story. When we see people slumped or with their arms crossed, we think things like, "they don't want to be here," or "they aren't comfortable with themselves." You can have the shiniest website or resume, but if your body says something different as you show up, it will affect how you speak and are perceived.

Passive, Active, and Neutral Posture

If you don't understand how to keep a neutral pose, your body will give you away. Try these exercises to learn how to ground your body and to align it with the story you want to tell.

The Passive Pose: Stand up, and bring your feet closer than hip distance apart. Take all your weight and bring it to the front of your feet, toward your toes. Let your knees get loose and tilt your hips and pelvis back. Allow your upper back to naturally follow this action, which makes your shoulder and head roll forward, with your eyes gazing toward the floor. Let your arms hang or cross them in front of you. How does it feel? Is it similar to how you normally stand?

The Active Pose: Okay, now wiggle that stance out. Stand up straight again and widen your legs to slightly wider than hip distance apart. Bring your weight to your heels. Keep the back of your legs and knees straight, push your pelvis forward, and bring your shoulders up and strong. Your head is looking straight ahead. Your arms can hang or go on your hips. How does this feel? If someone were to look at your posture right now, what would they say? They might say powerful. They might say confident. But this is a fake power pose. People who enter the room like this can look like they have something to say, but don't care what anyone else has to say. It gives the impression that you have it all figured out and you'll talk at me, but never with me.

The Neutral Pose: Stand with your feet hip distance apart. Put your weight evenly to the front and back of your feet. Keep your knees slightly loose and put your pelvis in a neutral position. Roll your shoulders back; your neck is straight and you are looking straight ahead. Your arms are at your side. This is a neutral body pose. This pose gives the impression that you want to be in the room, that you're confident and open for conversation.

There is a time and place for each of these poses, but if you're carrying yourself in the extremely passive or extremely active pose, your body is telling a story to everyone who meets you. Make sure your body's story matches what you're saying. Watch what your body does. It's always sharing.

Video Posture

It's likely that your next work opportunity will start with video. It might be a video interview, a conference call, or a video you make as part of sharing your career brand. People are quicker to judge you based on your appearance, tone, surroundings, and posture than based on your voice, so it's very important to pay attention to how you are coming across. Here are a few ways to look better on video.

Love the Lens: Video is an eye-show, so when the camera comes on, look at the lens, not at yourself or the other person. I often cover the computer screen with a piece of paper, so that I only look at the lens. Make eye contact with the lens and smile with your eyes. It might help to place a picture of someone you love just behind the lens camera to help keep your eyes high and light.

Seating: Sit on a chair that allows your feet to be flat. Sometimes when we're nervous we bounce our legs, and that bounce can seem exaggerated on video. Place your feet flat on the ground to stop yourself from bouncing. This also ensures you are not lopsided on the screen. Place your hands in your lap when you're not talking.

Head Posture: When you're truly listening to someone, your mouth is slightly ajar—not wide open, but slightly open. Having your mouth open a bit when the other person is talking also allows you to emote and look involved. Nod slightly where appropriate.

What's behind You: Your background says a lot about you. Ensure that it's telling the same story that your body is telling. If you talk about yourself as a creative person, have artwork behind you to help confirm that story. If you share stories about how organized you are, don't set yourself up where they can see your messy kitchen. Look at your screen and background and ask, "Does this background match the story I tell about myself?" If not, change it. Some people simply buy a tall room divider and use that as a background.

Directing Your Eyes: Stick any notes you are using to the edges of your computer screen or on the wall behind it. This will ensure that your eyes keep looking up. Your eyes are energy. Looking at the lens and looking up tells a story of being interested and engaged. Downward eyes or eyes looking at the screen or keyboard tell a story of disinterest and distraction—or even low confidence.

LEARN THE ELEMENTS OF A GOOD STORY

Beyond your posture, there are the actual stories you're going to tell. In a networking meeting, you'll introduce yourself by naming your skills and what you hope to do. This should be a story. Many professionals get the idea of a story mixed up with the idea of an example. An example is static. But a story has details, emotions, change, tension, time, and action. Here's how to weave in the elements that turn a static example into an incredible story.

Detail

Detail helps the listener imagine what you're saying. It allows the story to grow in their mind. Say a potential client asked me to share how I help people write their resumes, and I said: "I lead them through a method and they end up having a resume they love."

There isn't much for the person to imagine in that. I didn't give them enough details. But if I said, "When people come to me they say they've applied to over 60 jobs and they don't know what's wrong with their resume. For our first meeting, I sit with people and listen to their stories. I help them see what is significant about them by highlighting words and asking questions. From there, I..."

Even with that answer, my right client is imagining someone who is confused and getting help from me, and imagining how it would feel to be listened to and guided. So I add in detail about the 60 jobs, sitting together, listening, and highlighting words to help the client imagine me doing the work. Ideally, they are imagining themselves getting that service.

The feeling that someone gets when listening to a story with well-selected details lasts long after the story. They have had an emotional reaction.

When you select details to share, ensure they're universal and easy for the listener to imagine. If I had said something like "I help them write a two-page functional resume that gets them job offers" I might confuse a listener who doesn't know what a functional resume is or looks like.

The Five Senses

Once you've mastered adding in details, see if you can build your story out further by trying to evoke sight, touch, sound, smell, or taste. This works best if you try to focus on just one sense at a time. When you evoke a sense in your listener, they'll remember your story for longer, especially if they've experienced something similar themselves.

One of the first stories I wrote that gained popularity on LinkedIn evoked the senses. Here it is:

I made it to the third interview stage. A meeting with the VP.

We spoke in her corporate office for ten minutes. Then she said, "Part of this job requires you to do presentations. I'm going to get a glass of water, and when I come back, you can do one for me. It can be on anything." Then she left.

All I could think of was the presentation I had done the day before.

She came back into the office. "Okay," she said, "let's see your presentation."

I stood up, pen in hand, and said, "I'm going to teach you how to check for head lice. The first part is to use a comb to separate the hair to view the scalp." I mimed with the pen as if it were a comb checking a child's scalp. "As you're checking for head lice, reassure the child that anyone can get lice."

For three minutes, I stood in the fanciest office I had ever been in and explained the art of lice detection. I got the job.

Months later we laughed about it. She said, "If you had the guts to stand up and pantomime checking for lice, I knew you could teach anything."

As your career grows, it's no longer enough to answer questions. You have to demonstrate value and skills too.

After I posted this, many people wrote to share stories about their own experiences dealing with lice. They said they got itchy just reading the post. But even more people shared stories about knowing how it felt to be out of your element at a job interview. I've had people bring up that story months after I told it to them, saying, "I totally feel you." That's what you want: to leave them feeling something.

Action and Change

Your story needs to have action—something needs to change between the beginning and the end. Usually in your career stories, you are the one taking action. You are the main character; the story begins with something unusual happening, and then you describe (ideally with detail and evoking the senses) what action you took. The story ends with a positive result or lesson. Before you tell a story, whether online, in person, or on paper, first think about it and pay attention to the actions that you took. If you realize that someone else took more action that you did in your story, choose another one.

Your career stories are meant to help people understand how you work. Telling a story in which another person takes action based on your advice might work in the specific case of selling your leadership skills, but more often than not you will want to make yourself the main character.

Beginning, Middle, and End

The stories you use to sell yourself should, as much as possible, have a traditional structure. Yes, there are debates about how a story can work even if nothing happens and there is no clear ending, but when you're using stories to sell yourself, stick with what people know. But do make sure your career stories have short beginnings and endings, and a long middle. You want to quickly name a situation, dig right into the action in the middle, then resolve it with one line.

Most often, you are sharing your career stories in short spurts. They might be social media posts or comments, a five-minute video, something you share in a group conversation at a networking event, or a story you tell during an interview. This is not the time for an audience to gather and settle in for a long tale.

AVOID THE THREE STORYTELLING MISTAKES

Using story as a career growth tool is different from sharing stories with friends or family. The interviewer is going to have a lot less patience. The next time you're telling a story and it falls flat, think about whether you made any of these three mistakes.

The Run-Around

This is something that happens a lot in videos and job interviews: You tell a clear story, but you keep repeating the lesson over and over. Doing this removes your story's impact and makes the listener feel like you think they're stupid. Instead of repeating the same lesson, trust that the listener got it the first time.

Asides

Every few sentences, you might make a side comment relating to what you just said. Doing this once or twice in a story can add interest and humor, but doing it too much can lessen the story's impact. Consider this story:

> I was the sales manager (but really had the duties of a director). Every month my team would meet the sales goals, but the CEO kept upping the expectation (understandable). We needed to make $100,000 in just three days (which seemed impossible) so I got together my five best guys . . . these are the guys that I'm friends with outside of work too. We fish together, drink together, and work well together and although I'm the manager, I don't act like I'm better or anything, lots of mutual respect. So I got these five guys together in a room and we started to plan out the strategy. They groaned at first . . .

The asides hurt the flow. In an interview you get points for the actions you take, so if you spend the whole time making asides, you'll get zero points and you might run out of time. Here are three tricks for staying on track.

Have a Lesson: For every question asked in an interview or while networking, ask "what are they trying to learn by asking this question?" That's your road map.

Trust in the Listener: Stick to sharing details that the person can imagine instead of adding your opinion. For example, instead of saying, "We needed to make $100,000 in just three days (which seemed impossible)," say, "We needed to make $100,000 in just three days, which was far beyond our usual goal of $20,000 a week." This allows the listener to create their own opinion and gain interest in the story.

Train with Limits: Practice telling a story you know well, but restrict yourself to saying two asides per story. This trains you to notice when you do it and to pivot back to details and action.

Leaving Out Key Details

Your job is to help people see how you can help them. The specifics are the magic of your stories—they help the listener imagine you doing the work. If you rush over the details, they'll have nothing to remember you by.

This matters not just for people looking for job-jobs, but also for entrepreneurs. Often, people aren't really buying a product, they're buying the feeling the product is going to give them. If you tell a story about helping another person or company reach the same goals that the listener wants, they're going to be drawn in. If you layer in details about how you did it, they can imagine themselves doing it as you tell it to them. A lack of details leaves a fuzzy impression. You want to leave a sharp impression.

Details that make stories stronger evoke the senses. The easiest way to do this is to add a visual detail. Instead of "I lead a team of people," you can say, "I lead a team of five people in their 20s who dress like they're in a GAP ad. They're new grads and each one wants to grow in the company; they're fun to manage." Or, "I manage a team of five senior managers who've worked with the firm for over ten years. More than once I've entered a boardroom and thought, 'They could be in an ad for a law firm TV series.'" Help the listener imagine where you've worked, who you've worked with, and how it felt to be there. Every story you tell should have at least one detail that evokes the senses.

The SOAR Method

A great way to make stories out of your skills is to use the SOAR method. Take one of your career stories cards and second blank index card. On the blank card, write the letters S O A R down the left-hand side.

- **S** is for situation. This will 5% of your story.

- **O** is for obstacle/opportunity. This will be 5% of your story.

- **A** is for action. This will be 80% of your story.

- **R** is for result. This will be 10% of your story.

Beside each letter on the card, break down the story on your career stories card into these elements, weighted to match the corresponding percentage.

Situation

Give this at most three sentences. It might sound like:

- I was working at a bank in Kenya and had just been promoted to manager.

- I was working at a radio station as a receptionist.

- I was a substitute teacher, but I mostly worked for one school.

Give just enough information for the listener to understand the situation, so they are grounded in when and where the story occurred.

Obstacle/Opportunity

This can be combined with the situation element, like so:

- I was working in a bank in Kenya and had just been promoted to manager when news of a currency change came in ...

- I was working at a radio station when an angry listener came into the office dressed like a goose ...

- I was a substitute teacher, but I mostly worked for one school. One day the principal called and asked if I could sub for two teachers in one day ...

Action

This is where you describe, in detail, the actions that you took. Here, you can linger, add details, evoke emotions, take subtle pauses, and play around a little. The cool thing is that because you've already been working on your stories and understanding yourself, this part of the work gets easier and easier.

Result

Wrap up your story by spending the final 10% on the resolution. Simply let the listener know what happened because of the actions you took.

Do this for every career stories card that is suited to the requirements of the job you are after.

PRACTICE YOUR STORIES

The best way to become a better storyteller is to tell stories. It's an active art form. You can't become a great storyteller by just listing notes on paper. You need to say your stories out loud.

To build up your storytelling skills, choose one story to work with—your favorite one from your career stories cards.

Tell this same story aloud to yourself every day for a week, and record it. Every day, switch the story up just a little bit:

- Start the story in a new place. This helps you notice where the action is.

- Add in a new detail. (Remember: the magic is in the specifics.)

- Play around with where you add in beats (pauses) to help build tension and let the listener imagine what you're describing.

- Say it in a whisper. Yell it. Say it like it's an email rant. Imagine telling it at an interview. Then try it again like you're sharing the story with someone at a bar.

- Treat your story like it's a gift to the world.

- Weave industry words into your story, keeping the action the same.

As you play around with how you tell your story, notice what new aspects you enjoy the most. Some people love to add in descriptions, others love adding in asides to their story. What's the most enjoyable for you? Whichever it is, that is your natural storytelling style, so respect and nurture it.

The next week, do the same with a new story, and so on. Once all of your stories feel refined, you can start sharing them.

TRUST YOURSELF

Everyone can tell stories. Yes, everyone—but it takes practice and effort. Commit to working with stories every day. Look for opportunities to share them online, in person, and in groups. The more you work with stories, the more you'll appreciate them. Falling in love with story work can make you a better listener. You'll notice the nuances of other people's stories, and try out new methods for yourself.

Stories also help you get better at noticing things. As you tune into finding the important details to share about your own work, you'll start to see the details of the world. You'll notice the color of doorknobs, the way paper sounds when you pick it up, and how the light hits your desk in the afternoon. You're not only becoming a better storyteller, observer, and listener, you're also ripe for becoming a creative.

Take some time to practice your stories. When you're ready, get out there and start connecting with others.

ACTIVITIES TO SUPPORT STEP 8

Visualization

Think about your career dream. Visualize how you spend your days. What is the work environment like? What kind of people are you working with or for? How do you get to work? What do you wear? How do you want to feel when you wake up? Now, write down the first five stories that you tell yourself about why you can't have a career like that. Then, create the story about why you do deserve to have a career like that.

Self-Interrogation

Question your negative assumptions. If you are currently telling yourself a story about how a certain skill you have is seen as negative, I invite you to write it down and examine it.

- Think about the times this skill has made things better.

- Ask yourself: How does having this skill help other people and companies?

- Write down why it's great to have this skill.

Then, try walking around your house like you're proud of this skill. Notice how you hold your body differently, how you are lighter. Try walking like this a few times a day.

Your Greeting

Quick! How are you currently introducing yourself at networking events? Write it down now:

_____

_____

_____

_____

_____

Is it memorable? Does it match the skills you identified in your career stories? Does it use any sector language? If not, how might you change it to show your new career brand?

Deeper Detail

Look at one of the stories from your cards. Does it have a detail that draws the listener in? If not, what detail could you add to help people see your story better?

Story Study

Think back to a short story you love, whether it was fiction or non-fiction. See if you can find a copy of it. Re-read it. Then read it again and see if you can pick out elements of where the author shares a detail that sticks with you. How do they build tension? What, if any, sense or emotion does the story evoke and how does it evoke it? Study it, then try re-writing one of your career stories in the same style.

Repetition and Rehearsal

Commit to telling a career story every day. It might be to someone on the bus, a co-worker, through a post on LinkedIn, or just to yourself in the mirror. You get better with every story you tell.

STEP 8 CHECK-IN

1   Have you been practicing your stories every day? How
    has that changed the way you share and hear stories?

2   Have you noticed people treating you differently now
    that you share stories and ideas more often?

3   Are there other story styles you are interested in trying?
    Try to attend a play or read a book to see if there are
    other story techniques you could weave into your work.

—

CONNECT WITH
YOUR PEOPLE

—

ONE OF THE best career boosters is to expand your network and experiences. Sometimes when we hang out with the same people who say the same things, we can't imagine our lives being anything but how they are. That's when you need to expand your point of reference.

This step asks you to start building a better connection with your community and target sector. If you have your career stories and know what you're awesome at, and you're practicing a contemplation program, that's great. Don't skip that work. But if you're not out sharing stories with people, no one else will know how amazing you are. So, how will they know you're available for new opportunities? A big part of having an incredible career is being part of something bigger than you. That means leaving the house.

FIND YOUR PEOPLE

This is the first step in a networking plan. After you've found your people, you can start to meet industry or sector people. To get started, get your calendar right now and reserve two nights every month for the next six months. Mark it as "connection time."

You might be thinking: who are my people, and why do I need them? When I say "your people," I mean people who fully understand you and the profession you are now in. There's a big chance you've gone through the previous eight steps completely alone, only motivated by your willpower and the need to create a career. You're incredible. But you can't build a career on your own. You're going to need fans, supporters, and advocates.

It's hard to put yourself out there even on a good day, never mind when you haven't experienced any successes. Your people are the ones who are not scared to see you succeed; in fact, they usually encourage it, and you help them as much as they help you. These are rarely the people attending free networking events; often, they're the ones speaking at really cool events that you honestly enjoy. You can find them on social media too.

What these people do is accept you purely for who you are. They see you trying to improve yourself and your career, and they listen to the good stuff and the bad stuff. This might sound like a best friend, but they're better than that—they get you, plus they have contacts and business smarts that help you out.

Here's the thing: they want you as much as you want them.

It's a bit tricky to find these people, but that's why you need to seek them out. I suggest searching social media for people who have a voice in your target industries. Not the company owners or executives, but the people who are planning and speaking at smallish events.

Who in your desired industry is making things happen? Go where they are. What are they writing about? Go read it and comment. Attend their online classes and talks. Go to those events with no goal or intention other than to find a new friend.

Doing this work helps you in two ways:

- You get to practice your most natural networking style, just by being an interested person.

- You get to know the people who make things happen, and help them do it.

Networking is not about getting to the top person right away. You probably wouldn't know what to say to them anyway. Instead, start slowly by working the edges of the industry, learning the ropes, making some friends and working inward. When you build new friends in new industries through a mutual respect of each other's work, you gain some social clout and industry insight. Networking is a long game.

If you already have a group of friends and professionals that understand and accept you, you're a lucky one.

You already know what it feels like to belong. If you don't have this yet, seek it out. It's one thing to know your own awesome, and another to feel confident enough to share it. Belonging helps.

CONNECT WITH OTHERS

At least once or twice a month, go out to where you'll be with other people. This could be a board game club, a networking event, a class, a conference, or coffee with a peer. This activity is your commitment to share stories and ideas with others—even small groups, say, one or two other people. The more you go out and meet people, the better you get at it, and the more people know what you're about.

From there, you can expand your network. Once you have some core people who get you, start going to places that are new to you. Marnie is a real estate agent who attends a new meet-up every week (though she did adapt her networking strategy when COVID-19 happened). She goes to events where she doesn't know anyone and introduces herself and asks questions. She knows that not everyone is looking to buy or sell a house, but she also knows that if the people she meets don't already have a realtor, they're going to call the one they know best—that's her.

Go to these events with the mindset of making just one or two new connections. You don't need to meet everyone. The purpose of this regular connection work is not to land a job or new business—that might happen—but to get used to putting yourself out there. It gives you a chance to introduce yourself and your work in a new way. The more often you are able to share your career story, the stickier your career brand gets. You and everyone else you meet will be saying the same things about you.

Pretty much every career and job search coach is going to tell you to need to network. It's how most people land jobs. If networking makes you cringe, I hear you. I used to feel that way too, and sometimes I get myself into situations where I still cringe, though a little less now.

MAKE A GREAT FIRST IMPRESSION

The two best pieces of networking advice I ever got came from a VP at an HR firm. We were to attend a networking event the next day together and she said, "Wear something people can compliment, and don't wear black." I ended up wearing black, but I added a statement necklace. I used to be a "fade into the background" kind of person, so the necklace was a big deal.

When I arrived, we hung up our coats together and she said, "Look at all the black coats here." She hung up her vibrant red coat and I thought, wow. She popped when she entered the room, and she could easily pick her coat out at the end of the event. "You should get a jacket in a different color," she said. Then she said, "Beautiful necklace."

I moved toward the beverage table, smiling at people as I passed. I got stopped twice by people who said, "Nice necklace." Then I got it. The statement necklace was not for me, it was for other people. What I was wearing offered them a natural conversation starter. It also showed I had personality.

Networking, while you are active in it, is not for you. It's for the other people. Your networking goal is to make it easier for other people to approach you.

After I got a cup of tea and a plate of fruit I found her at a table. She was talking with someone else. I drank my tea. The person she was talking with stood up to get a drink and the VP turned to me. "We should spread out. And try acting like a host," she said.

"A host?" I asked.

"Yes, pretend this is your event, your party. And your job is to make everyone feel welcome."

Again, that changed everything for me. Instead of wandering the room looking for a quiet place to hide or waiting for others to approach me, I looked for people who needed someone to approach them. I moved around the room, stopping to chat with anyone who was sitting or standing alone. I entered conversation circles when I noticed a lull. My job was to just make sure everyone felt welcome and was having a good time. And the best way to make people feel welcome is to give them your attention.

INTRODUCE YOURSELF IN A NEW WAY

People always worry about how to introduce themselves at a networking event. You don't have to worry, because you have your career stories cards. You know what you're great at and what you want to do next, and you've rehearsed your stories, so you're good at telling them. So that's what you'll do.

Even if you love the job you have, I recommend introducing yourself in terms of your skills or how you help instead of your job title. A job title doesn't always share the scope of your work and impact. There are some titles, like actuaries, that people don't even fully understand but are often too shy to ask about. If networking is about setting people at ease, make it easy for others to understand what you do, and to ask questions about your work.

Here are three ways this type of introduction can look.

Introduction A

If you are in a career transition, you could talk about what you are currently doing and what your goal is. It might sound something like this: *I am currently learning all I can about (enter thing that interests you) so I can (enter thing you want to do)*.

Here's how that could sound in action:

- I am currently learning all I can about Winnipeg tourism, so I can get a job marketing our city.

- I am currently studying how content marketing works, so I can help small businesses get noticed.

- I am currently baking a cake every day to see if really want to be a baker.

If you use this version, be prepared to talk about the research you've been doing, along with some interesting facts. This will allow you to talk about your interests and future, instead of what you used to do.

Introduction B

Instead of talking what you're learning, you could say what you help people do. This can come from your career stories cards. It sounds like this: *I help (say who you help) to (say what you help them to do).*

Here are a few examples:

- I help people manage their finances.

- I help people use their stories to land ideal work.

- I help companies land big contracts through deep listening and highly developed negotiation skills.

You may get questions about how you help, so be prepared to talk about that. This is a fun one because you immediately show that you're interested in helping others, and it's not all about you.

Introduction C

There is a chance that you will be networking before you have career clarity yet. In this case, you can be honest: *I am trying to figure out where to go from (name previous role).*

Here's how this type of introduction might sound in practice:

- I am trying to figure out where to go next from being a master marshmallow maker.

- I am trying to figure out how to use my arts degree.

- I'm testing a few things.

This takes the pressure off having to figure out your next step, and allows space for conversation. It shows vulnerability, which can be attractive.

TALK ABOUT WHAT MATTERS

Ramone was going to an open house at a tech company in Toronto. We met to plan out his networking strategy. He had attended open houses before and nothing had come from his efforts. In the past he would show up, tell his elevator speech to anyone, ask about jobs, then leave. This left zero impression.

We created a strategy where he would not talk about himself as much. I said, "Ask the employees questions about the new space. Ask them what they like about working there, and start conversations that have nothing to do with the work." He agreed and attended the event.

The next day I asked Ramone about the event. He said, "Kerri, it was great. I went in and noticed a bunch of programmers like me were speaking with an employee about job openings. So I joined the group."

"Cool," I said, "what happened?"

"Well, they were all talking about their experience so I talked about mine too. And then I left."

I said, "So, how did you look different than any other programmer there?"

He went quiet.

I repeated the question: "What personal connection did you make with one of the employees that is usable today?"

He said, "I guess I didn't make any."

When you network and behave like every other person, you blend in. Being an incredible networker is not about talking business that day, it's about making the connection. When you make a strong connection with someone and they enjoy talking with you, they'll continue to talk to you.

My network is strong because whether I'm talking with someone in person or on LinkedIn, we talk about things outside of business. We talk about shows we like, books we're reading, our pets, and our hairstyles. We build rapport and trust. Then, if I need something from them, or if they need something from me, we do business.

The best way to make a great impression is to be present, make eye contact, ask questions, and be sincere. You don't need to flatter, just show interest. It's so rare that someone actually listens to someone else that it's a treat to experience. It feels incredible.

A great move to make at a networking event is to connect someone with new people. If you talk to someone and they say they're into AI, then later you meet an artist who wants to work in AI, you could say, "Hey, have you met so-and-so? They work in AI. I'll introduce you to them."

This makes you look like a great listener and a great connector. I love having connectors in my network.

PREPARE SOME CONVERSATION STARTERS

If you're taking on the role of host, you're going to be the one starting conversations.

You could talk about the event or space. A simple, "Hi, have you come to this conference before?" is a fine introduction. You could also say something about the room, the location, the sector, or anything you see in the present space. Try to keep it positive.

You could also talk about something you see on the other person. Remember the impact my necklace had? Try "Nice bag," or, "I have those same boots." Stay away from making comments about their body. I have used this technique online too. I'll connect with someone on LinkedIn and comment on a post they made or how I like the angle of their headshot. The practice of noticing others is worth practicing. Being seen feels good.

I have a casual networking style, so I'll seek out the person who looks the least comfortable and say, "You look the type of person who was told to come to a networking event, but doesn't love them. Did I call that right?" This can be disarming. I've met great friends (go, introverts!) this way.

You can also talk about something you read or saw. Read up on the latest positive news stories before you attend the event. Then, if you make eye contact with someone, you can say, "Hey... did you hear that story about the dog who saved the kitten from falling in the well?"

The art is in looking at how a person is behaving, then saying the opener that you feel will work best. For sure I have approached the wrong person and found myself in a dull conversation. When that happened, I would talk with them for a while, then say, "It was great talking with you but I promised myself I would meet three new people at this event, so I'll see you later."

In my experience, the more senior or respected the person, the more they enjoy casual conversations. If a person is known for a particular position or company, you can guarantee that they get asked about it all the time. You could start a conversation by asking something different, like, "What's the most meaningful thing you've done this week?" Then, listen to the reply.

If you're talking with someone and you notice the conversation winding down, you can always ask, "Hey, what social media are you on? I'd like to connect beyond this." If they are active on social media, they'll tell you; they may also give you their email or number.

It's Not Just about New People

Networking is not always a matter of connecting with people you haven't met yet. It's also about nurturing relationships with people you already know. This might mean scheduling coffee and lunch dates. Sometimes, it's a quick email. Often we can neglect the people in our network until we need them. It's hard to get someone to be your reference or make an introduction when you haven't spoken in years.

People you know outside of your target sector are important too, especially if you decide to be an entrepreneur. I thought most of my clients would come from outside my network, but my first clients were all referrals from people I knew before I was a career coach. They worked with me when I was employed as something different, but they knew my personality and work ethic. Don't be embarrassed to reach out to people from even ten years ago—they may be the link you need to land ideal work.

DIVERSIFY YOUR NETWORK

In many sectors, people tend to stick with their own kind, and often their own race. This was realized by many when there was increased attention on the Black Lives Matter movement in the spring and summer of 2020. On #BlackOutTuesday, people on Instagram blacked out their squares for a day and were encouraged to share posts from Black voices. After that day, people from multiple sectors—including interior design, sustainable clothing, advertising, and skincare—shared that they had not been aware of how white their sector and network was. In a matter of days, Black business owners were celebrated, their names were shared, and people promised to be more aware of including BIPOC voices. If you are in a homogenous network, it's worth thinking about and working to address. People from cultures different from yours can be your people too.

If you do discover that all of your colleagues, collaborators, and friends are of the same race, look to expand your network. If you have the power to organize events, conferences, or leadership teams, look to make them diverse and share opportunities—especially if you are white. Make the effort to seek out new perspectives and experiences in your field. This is not only a human move to make, it's also a wise career move. Your silence or inaction is part of your career story too. We are better together.

FOLLOW UP

Meeting new people is great, but you also have to think about what you do after you've met them. After each networking event, spend some time going over who you met, and consider how you're going to nurture those relation-ships. Did you talk about a topic that you could send them an article on? Could you introduce them to someone you know? Is there a project you'd like to do with them? Think about what you'd like to have happen next and plan from there. If you don't exactly know, then just follow up with a "Hey, it was great to meet you. I'd love to stay in touch."

Set a reminder three to six months from that for when you'll reach out again. Meeting new people is easy; having them be active in your life is another thing.

STRATEGIZE YOUR NETWORKING

Before you attend any event, do some minor research about it.

First, determine who you will be at the event. Will peo-ple already know you, or are you totally new to them? I carry myself differently if I know people will already be familiar with me and my work. I don't need to worry about conversation openers because I know people will approach me. I do have to think about *how* they know me, though. If I go to see a play, a lot of writers and actors will know me, but they know me for my theater work. So instead I'll plan what I'll say about myself and my work now.

You might be attending an event where you want to meet a specific person—say, you're going to a fundraiser and you know the hiring manager of the company you want to work at is on the board. Determine why you want to meet them. What do you know about them already? What will you say to them when you are introduced? You don't need to memorize a script, but know the gist of what you'll say.

Make a few notes about why other people are attending. What do they hope to get out of the event? How might you help them reach those goals? Then, determine what your own ultimate goal is in attending this event. Is it to meet new people? To practice some networking intros?

Finally, make it meaningful. Define what difference attending this event or meeting someone new will make in helping you reach your career goals. Why does it matter?

ACTIVITIES TO SUPPORT STEP 9

Posture
Continue to practice your body language. Every day, stand in the mirror and watch how you hold your body. Practice standing straight, with your body weight equally balanced between both feet. You can even practice introducing yourself and talking without crossing your arms or putting your hands in your pockets.

Event Planning
Choose one or two networking events to attend. If you can vary the audience, one could be a casual meet-up and one could be a conference. Plan how you'll introduce yourself and what you'll wear to each one.

Introduction Refinement

Choose one new way to introduce yourself and write it out here:

_____

_____

_____

_____

_____

Practice saying it aloud so that it rolls off your tongue when you do it in a real situation. Ensure you use the words and terms you researched in Step 6. If you really like your new introduction, change your LinkedIn headline to match it.

Skills Modeling

Go back to your career stories cards and look at your top skills. How can you model those skills in how you network? For example, if one of your top skills is helping people, be sure to model this in your networking. Listen to people and offer to help them. Networking is modeling your career stories beyond the cards.

Story Preparation

Again, go back to your career stories cards. Choose two that are appropriate to tell at networking events. People love stories. If you're expanding your network through social media, how could you share these stories in a post or article?

Reconnect

Make a list of 20 people in your network that you haven't spoken to in years. Write each of them an email or call and ask them how they are. You can even set up an in-person or video meeting if it feels appropriate.

Diversity Check

Think about the people in your network, the people you follow, share ideas with, collaborate with, refer work to. Make a list of 20 of your closest influences and partners. Are they all white? Are they all male? Are they all from the same neighborhood? If everyone around you tends to look the same, seek out new people to follow, collaborate with, and support.

Networking Plan

Choose an event to attend and make your networking notes. What do you know about the other attendees already? What will you say to them when you are introduced? Remember: you don't need to memorize a script, but you should know the gist of what you'll say.

STEP 9 CHECK-IN

1   What have you done to expand your network and find some inside people?

2   Do you feel a sense of belonging in this industry yet? If yes, who are your support people to keep connecting with? If no, what will you switch up to get an in?

3   What has been your most successful networking intro so far? How could you improve it?

—

SELL YOURSELF

—

OUR ACTIONS BECOME part of our career brand. If we're always late and rude, that becomes what people know us for. You can't snatch a personal brand from the sky and say, "I am this new thing now"; it comes through in your actions. You already know what's important to you from doing the first four steps, and the sixth step gave you clarity on your target. Always have this larger story in the back of your mind. This is what you're modeling in every interaction with others, whether on paper, in person, or online.

Remind yourself: what is my career brand?

You are great at (career stories skill 1), (career stories skill 2), and (career stories skill 3), and you're looking to (name the job/industry/target).

Be deliberate about your personal brand. Commit to and model those skills in all situations until everyone is saying the same thing about you.

In this step, you will go back to your career stories cards and plan out how you're going to model those attributes everywhere. How can you show your top skills online, in person, in your resume, in interviews, at home, at the office, and even while grocery shopping?

Suzie was waiting at the chiropractor's office for an appointment when the HR manager of a company she had applied to came in—Suzie recognized them from their LinkedIn photo. She waited a moment, then introduced herself and said she had applied for a job at the company. They talked for a few minutes, then the chiropractor came out. When he saw them speaking, he said, "You two know each other? I always thought you'd get along." Suzie said goodbye to the HR manager and went into her appointment. On her way out, the HR person said, "It was great to meet you. Check your inbox—it would be good to talk more."

Suzie modeled her personality consistently everywhere, so her career brand was on point when she needed it. How are you showing up at all the places you go? Is it consistent? If not, identify where you need to build it up again.

WRITE THE PERFECT RESUME

When I first heard the word "resume," I fell for it hard. It felt fancy and French, and it rolled off my tongue ... *res-u-me*. I'm a bit romantic about them, because they are the only two-page document I know that can change someone's life while telling their professional story.

I was disappointed when I saw an actual resume for the first time, and when I was taught to write one by copying out phrases provided by my teacher. Resumes don't need to be boring or full of phrases no one wants to read. And you can absolutely write your own.

Here's what I believe about resumes:

- They are beautiful documents that share your very best stories.

- They are "start again" documents. Resumes are a place to hold and celebrate your favorite professional stories that can help you start again, not stay stuck or bring you back to work you don't enjoy.

- Everyone can write their own resume and have it work.

- A big part of resume writing is what you learn about yourself in the process.

- You tailor your resume for every job.

- It's not as boring or hard as it seems.

- Depending on your target position, you can have a lot of fun with it. You can lay it out like a modern magazine, add color, or play with fold lines.

- A resume system is the easiest way to keep track of your accomplishments. It is a working document that you keep updated, so you never need to be in a crunch to write one.

I'm going to show you how to write a great resume, and I'm going to make it as simple and joyful as I can. We're going to build it from the bottom up.

Before we start, there are few things you need to know:

- There is no such thing as a generic resume. You need to tweak every one you send out. Every job and company needs different things, even if the job title is the same. You'll have a better chance if you tailor your resume.

- One of the hardest playwriting rules to learn was "cut what you love." This works for resumes too—sometimes, in order to get it to work, you have to make some tough edits. You'll survive.

- This is going to be a zillion times easier for you if you have a job ad to work from. I recommend using two sources for your resume writing: your career stories cards and an ideal job posting. Go to a site like Indeed or LinkedIn Job Search. Search for job postings that are similar to what you want to do, and select two or three to work from.

- Entrepreneurs should also have resumes, especially if you're going to be submitting proposals to corporations. Go for the reverse chronological or functional style (more on this difference starting on page 223). You might also add an extra page that lists the types of projects and project scopes you have done. If you're not creating proposals for companies, having a networking resume ready can't hurt (I'll explain this type on page 226).

If you have a strong network and plan on emailing or physically handing your resume to people, you won't need to worry about format so much. But if you know you will be applying for jobs online, you'll need a resume that works well with an Applicant Tracking System (ATS). This is a software application that some companies use to scan resumes before they get passed onto the hiring people. Each ATS is different, but here are some general rules:

- An ATS cannot generally read anything in a text box, column, or table. This means you'll need a super minimal layout choice. All those pretty templates on Pinterest won't work.

- An ATS is programmed to locate certain words. You should tailor your resume every time for every company, using those words. It isn't as daunting as it sounds. Ideally, you're only applying for jobs you want, and it'll be minor tweaks.

- Your resume will still be read by human eyes. So, it's a balancing act of making it robot and human friendly. Don't just load it with keywords or the hiring person will know what you've done. Using stories in your resume keeps it human.

All of the advice that follows assumes that you are designing your resume for an ATS.

TURN YOUR CAREER STORIES INTO ACCOMPLISHMENTS

All right, this is the fun part. We need to conform all of your career stories so that they read like accomplishment bullet points. If you have a career stories card that you absolutely know you would never use on a resume, you can skip it. But you'll want at least three or four to work with.

Why? Because while your career stories likely don't have the keywords the company is looking for, your resume still needs to be interesting for the human who reads it. Your career stories cards keep it real.

Also, once you learn the secret of ATS resumes and how truly easy it is to customize a resume, it can be a bit too tempting to become a full-on chameleon. It's easy to start losing sight of your career brand. Your career stories cards keep your resume grounded in that brand.

Creating an Accomplishment Bullet

Accomplishment bullets are simply your career stories in a specific resume format. They look like this:

- Led a resume workshops for 18 executives that helped them understand and communicate their strategic advantage to potential employers. Shortened their unemployment period by six months.

It always starts with a verb, known here as an action word. Then you describe what you did and the result. Sometimes you mention the result at the end, and sometimes up front. Here's the first version:

- Surpassed all previous YOY revenue records (28% increase) during first three years by combining functional operational knowledge with mindset exercises.

And here's the second:

- Combined functional operational knowledge with mindset exercises, which resulted in surpassing all previous YOY revenue records—a 28% increase within the first three years.

For each career story, decide what action word is appropriate. You can use your own words or look at the job ad to see what verbs the company uses. Then, add more details to the bullet. Who did you help? How did you improve things? What are the specific details of the story?

Finally, add in the result.

Good and Bad Accomplishment Bullets

Not all accomplishment bullets are created equal. A bad accomplishment bullet is something like this:

- Trained and supervised staff.

This is an *awful* accomplishment. It's not even an accomplishment. But bullets like this can be found on thousands of resumes. Here's why it sucks:

- We don't know how many staff.

- We don't know what you trained and supervised them to do.

- We don't know if you were successful at training or supervising them.

This statement could describe training and supervising a staff of three at a community center summer camp. Or it could be about training and supervising 100-plus air traffic controllers.

Add that type of detail to help the hiring person understand the depth of your experience. Here's how that could help each of those examples:

- Trained and supervised three community center summer camp staff.

- Trained and supervised over 100 air traffic controllers.

These are okay. But we still don't know what you trained them as, or what the result was. So, add in more details:

- Trained and supervised three community center summer camp staff on how to manage groups and perform CPR. The staff felt equipped to handle any simple emergency and there were no accidents reported that summer.

- Trained and supervised over 100 air traffic controllers on how to manage stress while on the job. Designed role play scenarios to provide real-time feedback. This staff cohort reported lower levels of stress than previous graduates.

The best advice I can give about what makes a great accomplishment statement is to write it out, then ask yourself: "So what?"

Seriously, *so what* that you trained three staff and there were no emergencies?

How do you defend it? If your response is, "Well, in the previous three years, there were concerns from parents about preventable accidents." Then add that into the bullet point. Like this:

* Reduced accidents at a summer camp program from five per year to zero by training and supervising three community summer staff on how to manage groups and perform CPR. The staff were equipped to handle any simple emergency.

See? Asking *so what* helps. The people reading your resume are asking that too.

Sometimes you might have a story that can't be fit into one accomplishment statement. You can always add some sub-bullets, like this:

* Developed and implemented a new mail sorting process, which:
  - Reduced opening timelines by two days
  - Set the new mail sorting record in New York and single facility record for sales per square foot

    - Provided a new model as the SOP for all new mail openings in the US

You wouldn't want every bullet point to have sub-bullets, but two or three per resume is fine.

USE JOB ADS AS A KEYWORD RESOURCE

The easiest way to find the kind of skills and accomplishments an employer is looking for is to draw from a sample job ad or two. Collect a couple of job ads from the role or sector you're going for. You'll notice it likely has several parts:

- Company introduction (usually a blurb about the company and overview of the role)

- Job description (usually a bulleted list of what you'll do in the job)

- Qualifications (a shorter bulleted list of required education, skills, and certifications)

- A blurb at the end that talks about their culture

Copy and paste the text of one ad into a blank document. Then, read over the text, looking for words that show up more than two times. These are often your keywords. Highlight them however you like.

Here's a quick test. Read the job ad that follows and circle the words you think are keywords. (Hint: there are seven.)

The role of the master marshmallow maker is to make, create, and package exceptional marshmallows. Our marshmallows are not just a food to be burned over fire. They are an exceptional and unique experience. You will work with a team of three other experts to make marshmallows from scratch. You will help to create new designs and shapes as part of a team. Your fine design eye will be also benefit our design team to see how the creations you make could translate into wider brand marketing.

Duties:

· Create and make delicious marshmallows from scratch.

· Collaborate with a team of other makers to create new marshmallows.

· Test out new designs in the kitchen, then communicate the design features to the marketing team for taste tests and marketing opportunities.

· Keep the kitchen and work area clean.

· Notify kitchen manager when new supplies are needed.

· Act as ambassador for the company at local events.

Qualifications:

· Culinary arts diploma
· 5 years of experience working in a commercial kitchen
· Organizational skills

- Communication skills
- Experience testing new food products would be preferred

Did you find seven keywords? Here they are: marshmallow, make, create, exceptional, collaborate, test, and team.

If you were writing a resume for this job ad, you would want to make sure to include all seven of these words. But beyond matching their keywords, you also want to show this company that you have experience in the skills they are looking for. There's an easy trick for that.

For each of the statements above, imagine they start with: "Tell me about a time you…" For example, the first duty on the job ad says "create and make delicious marshmallows from scratch." So, write this down: "Tell me about a time you created and made delicious marshmallows from scratch."

Now, review your accomplishment bullets to see if you already have a match for what they're asking for. If you don't, write a new response about a time you created and made delicious marshmallows from scratch. Write out the story first, then turn it into an accomplishment bullet.

If you've never made marshmallows from scratch, but you have made something else from scratch, write about that. Think of the closest experience you have to doing the specific task they ask for. (Take note, though: if you find that you have no related experience for the first six things the job ad asks for, you may want to try going for another type of job first, to start gaining that experience.)

Keep doing this for the first eight to ten bullet points in the job ad. If you want to write examples from the qualifications section, you can do that too. By the end, you'll have a variety of specific examples for each of the three types of skills a company will typically request:

- Hard skills: skills you learned or earned with school or experience

- Soft skills: often, these are teamwork, communication, and organizational skills

- Technical skills: programs or specialized skills that you need training for

The difference between hard and technical skills can be a little vague, but you can learn to differentiate them. For example, I'd call computer programming a hard skill, but knowing CSS a technical skill.

BE SPECIFIC, AND NEVER GENERALIZE

I've taught resume writing long enough to know there is resistance to writing specific stories. What I commonly hear is, "But I have done this work hundreds of times. Why would I only talk about one specific instance on my resume?"

Here's why: it has more impact, and it's more memorable.

If you were looking to hire someone to teach a resume writing workshop for IT professionals at your workplace and you requested that interested parties send in a proposal, which of the following people would you remember?

- Person A: Led resume workshops for thousands of people over a 20-year period.

- Person B: Led a resume workshop to a group of 20 IT professionals at the Mosaic Company. Adapted the workshop for their sector, including how to use technical program expertise in a resume. Received fantastic feedback from participants and management, and was invited to come back three years in a row.

In these examples, Person A shows they have done it for long time. Person B gives you an exact example of when they worked with the type of people you work with. You are more likely to go with Person B, and you are more likely to recall their story. You know that their one example is a universal example. If the resume writer is getting called back three years in a row, you can infer that they are doing other workshops as well. There is magic in the specifics.

If you can tell a specific story about the work you did, strong example after strong example, the hiring people are going to call you. People stop themselves from landing great jobs because they go too wide, and try to include everything. The hiring people just need to know you have experience in the work they are hiring for.

Your resume is not a career obituary. It doesn't need everything you have ever done. It is a summary of the work experience you have that is relevant to the reader.

I have a dog who dislikes having her nails trimmed. She tends to thrash around when you touch her paws—she's a rescue dog and I think her paws might have had frostbite in the past. There is one groomer that can handle her, but they are 40 minutes out of town. Often, my partner and I would plan a vacation or short trip to the woods every three months, and board her there for a weekend.

Unfortunately, the last time she was there she had a health concern and had to come back early, and they hadn't trimmed her nails yet. I started looking for a local groomer, and while many places said things like "in business for 15 years" and "we are a certified pet stylist," only one led with "we specialize in working with fearful and sensitive dogs." That's who I called, and I didn't question that they cost more than other places. They solved my problem exactly.

The same principle works in your resume: show the company how you have solved their exact problem before. They'll call you.

Five Tips for Easier Resume Writing

1 **Create a distraction-free zone.** Turn off social media and your phone so you can focus on this work. Resume writing is hard, and distractions will quickly take you away from the work.

2 **Work on one accomplishment at a time.** Set a timer for 15 minutes per line to help motivate you and stay focused.

3 **Wear something you feel amazing in (that's comfortable).** If you wear something that you'd never want anyone to see you in, what kind of energy are you bringing to what you're doing? This is your career, and this is career-building work—wear something nice. It doesn't need to be expensive; I personally thrift for tops and pants that are comfortable and made of fabrics that make me feel alive: silk, linen, and quality cotton. Or, try a luxe writing robe, something that makes you feel fancy and wonderful. Write from that place. Play around with wearing shoes or indoor slippers. It gives weight to the work. I write better with shoes on. I edit better barefoot.

4 **Make a resume creation playlist.** If working in silence doesn't feel motivating, take an hour and create a playlist of music, preferably instrumental, that will help you zone into the work. Give it a fun name like "music for amazing career transitions" or the "dream come true playlist." I always play music when I write; I'm listening to some right now.

5 **Don't judge your work too early.** To start, you just need content to play with. Embrace the first crappy draft—all artists have them, and you can clean it up later.

BUILD YOUR KEYSTONE RESUME

All of this may seem like a lot of work, and honestly the first effort can be a bit burdensome. But as you create and collect your accomplishments, what you're making is a *keystone resume* that you can adapt as needed.

So, what the heck is a keystone resume? This is your master live resume. Mine is currently ten pages long. Every time I accomplish something in my career I add the story to this document. It also holds all of my old profile statements (more on this soon), along with all of the details of my courses, volunteer work, education (more on that coming too), and anything else from my professional background that may be useful in a targeted resume someday.

Having this document means that whenever I need a resume, I can look at what the hiring company wants and match it with stories I have already written. It becomes a simple copy-and-paste job. Merge a few keywords in and I'm gold.

Once you have a keystone resume that holds all of your accomplishments, education, and job titles, you can pull the most relevant information and build a simple, fresh resume that's custom designed for each job you apply to—and you can also use it to create your LinkedIn profile, proposals, bios, and social media or other content. Add a reminder to your calendar to add new bullet points to your keystone resume a few times a year. That way, you'll never have to scramble in a panic to put a resume together again. It takes effort to make this system, but once you've built it, you have it for life.

The future of work is here, and the best thing you can do to be prepared is to have an inventory of stories that back up your experience. You know what you're great at, and you can back it up with solid examples.

CHOOSE YOUR TARGETED RESUME FORMAT

Okay, you have all of your accomplishments and experience gathered together in your keystone resume, and you've spotted an opportunity you want to go after. That means it's time to pull out a targeted resume from your keystone resume.

The first step is to choose the appropriate resume format. I liken resume formats to a screenplay. Screenplays have had the same format for almost 100 years. While every screenplay looks the same on paper, you can tell a quality screenplay from a poor one once you start reading it. The format doesn't limit your creativity, it gives clear boundaries on what to share and where to share it.

There are five main resume formats, and they're each suited to a very specific type of situation. I know that the overwhelming amount of information out there on resume trends can be challenging, and that takes some of the excitement out of going after a position you're interested in. So let's break the five types of resumes down and make the choice simpler. You can find a guide to structuring the first four of these resume types starting on page 304.

Reverse Chronological

This style of resume starts with a list of your work experience from the past ten to 15 years, starting with the most recent position.

When to Use It: This is the most ATS-friendly type of resume. Use this type when you have relevant experience and/or the same job title as the position they are hiring for. It's also good if you're looking to land something slightly higher up than your current role.

Pros: The reverse chronological style is generally the most trusted by hiring people. You aren't hiding any dates or titles in a fancy format. This is also the easiest to make.

Cons: If you don't have relevant titles or work experience, it can hide your skills.

Choose If...

- You have work experience in the specific sector.

- You have had the same or similar job title as the one you are applying for.

- The accomplishments in your most recent job relate directly to the job.

- You're applying to a conventional organization, such as a bank or government body.

- You have more than six months doing relevant work.

Functional

If there is such a thing as a controversial resume style, this is it. I'm serious. Almost daily you'll see a LinkedIn post that says something like, "Someone asked me when they should use a functional resume. The answer is never."

This resume style highlights your transferable skills first and gives brief details on your work history on the second page. But be warned: if you have the experience, don't make them doubt you by using this resume style.

When to Use It: This is ideal for career changers and students. It allows you to highlight your skills and experiences first, then share job titles and dates on the second page. I used this type of resume to land an HR job after working in the arts. It can be useful for students who may not have had a job title, as it highlights the skills you earned through school, sports, and volunteering.

Pros: Highlights transferable skills that came outside of work or certain titles. Can be good for those who have job titles that don't match the depth or breadth of the skills they used.

Cons: Not as trusted. Some hiring people may think you are hiding something with this style.

Choose If...
- You have the skills to do the job, but in a different sector.

- You are changing career direction.

- It's not obvious from your job titles that you have relevant experience.

- You want to highlight skills earned through volunteer work or a past job instead of your most recent position.

Hybrid
This resume is a combination of the reverse chronological and the functional resume styles. It features your skills on

the first page, then gives details about your work experience. This can be a great format if you want to highlight some skills, but also show that you have relevant work experience.

When to Use It: When you're looking to progress in your career and have some incredible accomplishment stories to highlight.

Pros: It shows both your skills and your work history.

Cons: Usually the hardest one to write. Also, the format is longer, so you may find it difficult to keep your resume to two pages.

Choose If...
- You want to highlight skills but you also have relevant work experience.

- The accomplishments you want to highlight are not from your most recent job.

- You are moving to a new sector.

Networking
This is an ideal format when you're sharing your resume for a job informally. This is a one-page document that highlights a few skills and shows where you have worked. It piques the hiring person's interest, and encourages them to ask for more details.

When to Use It: Only when you have a connection to the hiring team or decision maker—it's ideal for connecting with people in your network for a casual drink or meet-up, or for when you have a friend who knows there is an opening at their company but they don't have many details yet. You can give them this resume and say, "I have a more robust one, but this has some of my highlights so you have something on paper about me."

Pros: It highlights a few stories without overburdening you or the reader. You can tailor it for the exact company and person because you know them. You can provide stories that might inspire the creation of a new job tailored for your exact expertise.

Cons: You should only share up to three stories, making it hard to write when you have a lot of skills. This could give the false impression that you have limited skills if the resume gets moved up the hiring ladder. You'll also need to be prepared to write a second, more formal resume if requested.

Choose If...

- There is no job ad.

- You're meeting someone about a role and want something on paper, but you don't want to offer something that's too stuffy.

- You're attending a job fair or open house.

Graphic

Graphic resumes look more like a magazine or collage than a resume. They're popular on Pinterest. They often contain color, graphs, and sometimes images. These resumes can be used to apply for jobs that are more creative, like graphic designer. They only work if you can email the document to a human being—they are not ATS compliant.

When to Use It: Typically when a large corporation is hiring a graphic designer or creative director, they still use ATS to parse the resumes. So, you might have one resume to get you through HR, then bring a graphic one with you to the interview. If you're applying to a smaller organization or startup, a graphic resume alone may work just fine. But remember that visuals do not replace quality stories. You still need to highlight career accomplishments and show your experience.

Pros: They look cool and show the hiring team your graphic and creative abilities.

Cons: Only use these when applying for creative design jobs. For other types of work, this kind of design can actually hurt your chances. They are also not ATS compliant.

Choose If...

- You work in a creative industry and you're applying to a human being instead of through an ATS.

CRAFT YOUR TARGETED RESUME

Once you've gathered all of your accomplishments in your keystone resume and you've picked the right format for the specific opportunity you're going after, we can start building your targeted resume. Every resume, regardless of format, has four main parts:

- Header
- Profile statement
- Work experience
- Education and training

Header

Your header must include your name, city, state/province, phone number, and email address. If you look awesome on LinkedIn, you can stick your LinkedIn URL in here. If you're more active on another site that your target company should see, add that in too.

How you design your header will change depending on your personality and preference. Browse samples and templates online to find one that suits you.

It's okay to add your education credentials to the end of your name if you're applying directly to someone. But if you're uploading to an ATS, don't. Some will turn them into your last name!

Also, another ATS warning: if you're applying for a job through an ATS, do not add your name using the header function of Word, as the system may not scan that area.

Just write it at the top of the document, with your contact information below it.

Profile Statement

This is the first thing that a hiring person will see on your resume. It's where they get a chance to quickly learn what you've done in your career and what your super skills are, and see a touch of your personality. I once read a study that said a hiring person spends 7.6 seconds looking a resume. So you want to catch their attention right away.

Your profile can be one to three sentences. I like to use three:

- The scope statement: This lets the reader know what you do, where you've done it, and who you've done it for.

- Your super skills: The second sentence lists three things you're really good at.

- Your personality: The third sentence can show a bit about how you work, or who you are.

Let's start with the first sentence: your scope statement. This is your professional title and how long you have done the work. Choose a job title that shows the reader what you are professionally. You can choose a title you've had, or a title you want. If you don't feel comfortable choosing a title, then provide an overview of the kind of work you've been doing.

Here are a few examples:

- Experienced roller coaster engineer with six years touring across North America.

- Career coach with over 15 years' experience leading workshops.

- Corporate change management professional with experience leading, managing, and analyzing change in small companies.

- Professional with two years' experience leading projects in the not-for-profit sector.

- Great communicator who has written and planned workshops for over 20 companies, including hospitals and museums.

Next comes your super skills. These can be the three skills you identified in your career stories cards. Some people choose to list two skills from the job ad and one skill from their career stories cards to ensure the resume works well for ATS.

Often, resume writers will include a mix of hard and soft skills. This helps show the reader how specialized you are in a field, and what you're great at.

Here are some examples of good second sentences:

- Valued contributor to IT projects through excellent communication skills, collaborative attitude, and not letting any projects drop.

- Track record for designing and executing memorable events.

- Known for building websites from scratch with little direction.

- Handled large amounts of data with ease and pleasure; made for overcoming data challenges.

- Developed relationships and trust with stakeholders that allowed for expansion.

What are you known for that this company would care about? Where does what they ask for in the job ad match with what you love to do? Share those things.

Finally, the third sentence is about how you work, or your personality. It could look like this:

- Works with commitment to client satisfaction and safety.

- Committed to lifelong learning.

- Works with enviable energy that helps motivate teams to reach a higher level.

- Works with a calming energy that increases workflow and communication.

- Gets the job done every time.

- Works quickly and with great focus—wears noise-canceling headphones.

- Obsessed with improving processes that help clients.

The last step is simply to put those three sentences together:

> Experienced roller coaster engineer with six years tour-
> ing across North America. Developed relationships
> and trust with stakeholders that allowed for expansion.
> Works with commitment to client satisfaction and safety.

Work Experience

In this section, you add the jobs you have had. This will
look different depending on the resume type you are using.
The work experience you list here should go back about
15 years, listing the job title for each position and date
range you worked there (years, but not months).

If you've had multiple titles, you can show it like this:

ABC Company   2013–2016
Manager, 2015–2016
- Accomplishment
- Accomplishment
- Accomplishment
- Accomplishment

Coordinator, 2014–2015
- Accomplishment
- Accomplishment

Sales Agent, 2013–2014
- Accomplishment
- Accomplishment

If you're writing a reverse chronological, hybrid, or networking resume, list your job title, dates, and company name. Then add the relevant accomplishments after it, like this:

Career Coach, Career Stories Consulting   2006–Present
- Accomplishment
- Accomplishment
- Accomplishment
- Accomplishment

Programs Officer, Government of Manitoba   2005–2006
- Accomplishment
- Accomplishment
- Accomplishment

If you're writing a functional resume, list the job titles, dates, and company names without any accomplishments, like this:

Career Coach, Career Stories Consulting   2006–Present
Programs Officer, Government of Manitoba   2005–2006

Education and Training

The education and training section goes on the second page, unless you are applying for an academic position. Typically, you only list the degree or course title, the school, and the dates. If you want to highlight specific courses, you can do it like this:

BA, Zoology, University of Zooland, 2016
Relevant courses:

- Zebra muscles and movement
- Walking patterns of apes eating licorice

Don't limit this section to just degrees—you can also add Massive Open Online Courses (MOOCs), self-led learning, and other short trainings. Ideally, you want to include at least one thing from the last two years. If you haven't done any training in the past two years, go sign up for a MOOC. They're fun, and they show that you're investing in your future.

WRITE AN IRRESISTIBLE COVER LETTER

Now that you have your targeted resume, you want to make sure it gets noticed. That's where your cover letter comes in. A cover letter is not necessarily meant to prove you are qualified for the job. It's meant to show why you should be considered and interviewed. You want to leave them with a memorable impression.

Cover letters stand out when they are written just for one specific company. In every position you apply for, tell the company why you want to work with them and what you can do for them. Writing an authentic cover letter is a built-in system to ensure you don't apply for jobs you don't want. If you can't come up with a deeper reason to work somewhere beyond the paycheck, it's not a great place to apply.

Here's what you need to do to make sure your cover letter is authentic, customized, and compelling.

Figure Out Why You Want the Job

Sometimes it's the job title or salary that attracts us to a position. That's okay. That's natural.

But to get the attention of the company hiring you, you need to go deeper and tell them *why you want this specific job, at this specific company.*

It's not about sucking up or giving false reasons. It's telling them why you want to work there. You need to tell them:

- Why you do the work you do.
- Why this job and their company will help you meet your mission.

This is a zillion times more interesting than "I am applying for the role of (name of job). I have 15 years of experience doing (task/role)." Some decision makers refuse to consider people who start their cover letter this way. They know you are applying for the job—that's obvious, because you literally have applied for it. Show them more. Start with something like this:

> My entire life has been about solving problems with my hands. It started by helping to fix stuff with my dad, and then I moved on to working with cars. When I saw the ad for a bus mechanic at Crosbey's Bus Life, I started researching and asking about your company. I found

out that you only hire the best, you have incredibly high standards, and you stand behind your work. The same goes for me.

Some common reasons why you are drawn to work a specific company might include:

- You heard they have a great culture from someone you trust.

- The work on interesting projects.

- They share your same values about high-quality work and professionalism.

- They'll help you reach goals you have been striving toward, and it's a win-win.

- They work with a clientele you want to work with.

If there is a company you are considering applying to, make a list of the top ten reasons you would like to work there, in the exact role you are going for. (Many of these will reasons link to your defined values from Step 3.) Write the reasons out here:

1 _____

2 _____

3 _____

4 _____

5 _____

6 _____

7 _____

8 _____

9 _____

10 _____

Choose the most compelling of these, and start your cover letter there. Most often, you will tell them this in the opening paragraph.

Define the Wants and Needs

Now, determine what the company actually wants and/or needs—both the hard skills and soft skills—and determine how you meet them. Here's how you do this:

- Review the job advertisement and identify the skills they are asking for.

- Categorize them into hard/technical skills and soft skills.

- For every hard and/or technical skill, write down the certificates, specializations, and number of years of experience you have.

- Write out a specific example of a time you used that skill (you probably already have this in your career stories cards).

- Select one or two soft skills highlighted in the posting and think of the best story you have of using that skill.

- Jot down the bones of that story. Then move on to the next step to identify which words you'll weave into the story for largest impact.

Find the Right Words

Organizations and industries often have their own common accepted language. You may have experienced this yourself: have you ever worked in a place where everyone spoke in a way that no one outside the organization would understand?

Many companies have insider words and phrases that have become so commonplace that they aren't aware they're using them. The awareness comes when someone shows up who is unfamiliar with the phrases and uses a different language. It's jarring, and company insiders may feel like the newcomer doesn't belong.

You can tell new people from seasoned. You want to sound seasoned in your cover letter. When you use the same words and phrases that people within the company and sector use, it makes the reader feel like you get them.

There are two ways to accomplish this: keywords and gist. Keywords are the words you found as you did your research in Step 6, and the specific ones you'll find now by identifying the keywords in the job ad. Could they be mentioned as your hard or soft skills? Can you use them as part of the story example you share? You don't want to copy and paste complete phrases, but do play around with adding them in strategically to have the letter look and sound natural.

Gist can be harder to pinpoint, as it's not exactly about the words in the ad. It's about looking at the role as a whole and asking, "What do they want? What is the underlying theme of this position?"

Look further than the job ad. Look at things the company promotes or what other employees are talking about. You're trying to get a feel for the culture to match the tone in your cover letter. If you send an ultra-polished and corporate-sounding cover letter, you may give the impression you are inflexible. Look for clues in the way they describe the role and company, and match that tone in your letter.

Identify the Barriers

If, while reading the ad or talking about the opportunity, you realize there might be barriers to getting hired, address these barriers explicitly in your cover letter.

I know, I know. You don't want to draw attention to them. But here's the thing: just by applying, you are already drawing attention to them. Your resume likely already shows one or more of many common barriers. These could include:

- Long periods of unemployment
- Multiple short terms
- No industry experience
- Some experience, but not as many years as the company desires

Instead of going ahead in the hopes that the hirer won't notice these barriers, address them outright. Give a brief explanation, positively phrased, about the perceived barrier. And don't be a schmuck about it! Don't say something like this:

> I know you are looking for someone with ten years of experience, but my three years is richer than most of the competition's.

Instead, try something like this:

> I don't have ten years of experience in this sector. I do have experience leading training sessions for senior leaders with a 98% satisfaction rating. One manager recently said, "You were born to do this. You do better than most of the master facilitators we hire for this work. You've found your niche." While I know this doesn't replace experience, if you are looking for someone to lead senior training sessions and meet sales targets, I can and have done that.

Identify any reasons you think they may not hire you. Do you lack experience or a hard skill? Do you have a patchy employment history? Then for each, think about how you will explain that it is not a reason not to hire you.

This is not about tricking a hiring person. It's about giving them a reasonable explanation for anything they might be questioning.

Do the Rest of the Research

You can add interest and credibility to your cover letter by demonstrating business acumen.

This doesn't mean taking something from their website and parroting it back to them. You can acquire business acumen by following the company on social media, setting up a Google Alert, reading articles in industry magazines, reading scholarly research about their industry, or talking to connected people to gather more information.

Once you've done this work, you can add a research sentence into your cover letter (often the fourth paragraph) to show your knowledge. Things you might mention could include:

- A recent trend in their industry
- A new product they have been developing
- A recent expansion
- An award they won
- A recent merger
- A competitor that came into the market

This line can be short—you can elaborate on your point at the interview. Here are a few examples of a good research line:

> With the recent arrival of your main competitor, Axel Fumes, it is important to have a person with (name a skill you have) on your team. I will bring that.

> I noticed that George Training was recently hired at ABC company. That will add a new element to the industry,

and I'd like to establish a new partnership between them and you that would see business flourishing.

I understand that last year you won the Top 10 Companies to Work For award. I would love to contribute to making sure you win again next year.

The point here is to set yourself apart from other candidates by showing your deep understanding of the industry and business.

Show Your Strategic Advantage

You have one more thing to think about: what will you do for the company if you get hired? It's not enough to tell them why you are super. Go the extra step.

Imagine you were the successful candidate for the position. Consider:

- What are some actions you would take?
- What results would you bring to them?

Make a list of these and add the best three or four to your cover letter. You can do this in two ways. The first is to tell them explicitly what you would do:

If I was the successful candidate, I would:

- Modernize your filing system, by examining the current system and making improvements.

- Train the staff in digital filing systems to ensure buy-in and consistent record keeping.

- Create a new system to improve processing time.

A tiny bit of caution: If you don't know the company well enough, this can sometimes be seen negatively.

The second option is to tell them about the kind of work they will get. That can look like this:

If I was the successful candidate, you would get:

- A professional who is devoted to best practices and keeps up to date on new research.

- Unwavering dedication to ensuring the client experience is memorable.

- My commitment to set and meet high standards. You have built a strong reputation and I will work to ensure it stays that way.

Put It All Together

Now you have all the elements you need to put together the perfect cover letter. Take everything you just prepared, then organize it into five paragraphs:

- Paragraph one: Tell them why you want to work in this role and company. Be creative about how you say this.

- Paragraph two: Tell them why you are qualified for the job, and share a specific story (this will probably come from your career stories cards). This paragraph is usually three to five lines.

- Paragraph three: If you want to add a second story example, do so here. You might choose to tell one hard skill story and one soft skill story, depending on the role.

- Paragraph four: Address any barriers. Insert a research sentence here, if you didn't use it in paragraph two or three.

- Paragraph five: Your closing sentence and strategic advantage. Use active language, and thank them for their time.

Then, add your sign-off:

Warmly/Sincerely/Kindly/Enthusiastically

Your name

Encl.

Once you've drafted your letter, review it alongside your list of keywords. Change the wording up to match the company's language and the gist of the job.

Finally, save the cover letter with the resume and a copy of the job ad. Remember: the cool thing is that your cover letter is the perfect cheat sheet for the interview screening call (more on that soon). It answers all of the questions they're likely to ask. You just need to stick to your career brand.

LOOK AWESOME ON LINKEDIN

We live in one of the best possible times to land ideal work. Never before have you been able to demonstrate your abilities for potential companies as easily as you can today. In the pre-internet days of job search, you had to physically mail or drop off your resume to be considered. Networking was important, but if you didn't know someone, and your resume was rough, you probably weren't going to land the job.

Now, there is an entire platform where you can not only share a profile of your accomplishments, you can also share content. Today you're not just being judged on a single two-page document; instead you can use sites like LinkedIn to share more about yourself: who you are, what you do, and what you know.

I'm going to talk specifically about LinkedIn because that's where a lot of people land work—and not just job seekers: LinkedIn is my number one place for getting new business leads from companies and individuals. But it's not the only professional networking site out there. Figure out where the decision makers you need to reach are hanging out online—then create a strategy to get their attention there.

Define Why You Are Using LinkedIn

Before you build your LinkedIn profile, you first need to determine why you're doing it. What do you want to have change or happen in your career or life?

- Do you want to make enough money from clients that you could quit your job?

- Do you want to land a job that gives you more joy?

- Do you want to feel heard and respected in your sector?

- Do you want to build your network?

Through my work I have helped people move from being unknown in their sector to becoming a respected thought leader. I've helped clients move from jobs they hated to becoming thriving business owners. And I've helped CEOs who wanted to change direction make that move intentionally. I've helped new coaches start winning clients. I've helped job seekers land jobs (even without a resume). Anything is possible. The strategy will change depending on your level and your target. That's the art of it.

It's always easier when we know the dream. This makes your strategy intentional and meaningful.

- What would change in your life if you met all of your LinkedIn goals?

- What is your big dream?

- Where do you want your career to go?

Take an index card and write out your reason. Do it like this:

I am on LinkedIn to (reason). And, by being on LinkedIn, I will go from (your current state) to (what you want to see happen by being on LinkedIn).

Here's an example:

> I am on LinkedIn to get clients for my cat-sitting business. And, by being on LinkedIn, I will go from having local clients to being known for helping other people set up their own cat-sitting businesses.

Hang the card nearby as you write your profile to keep your goal in mind. This goal may change over time. Some people start using LinkedIn to land a job. Once they land a job, they use LinkedIn to build their network or become a thought leader. As your goal changes, your strategy will change.

Use Your Career Brand to Craft Your Profile

You already know your career brand, including the skills from your career stories cards that you want to highlight. Open with some information on what you do and how long you've done it, or what's special about how you do your work. If you want something stronger and less direct to start, you can begin with:

- A quote
- Another kind of hook
- A story that highlights your favorite strengths

Here's how that cat-sitter might open their profile:

> Work hard, play hard is my life motto. Throughout my career as a cat whisperer, I have worked to understand

clients and solve their problems. But I also know when to take a break. I didn't build my business to take over my life.

After your opening, you can share stories, give examples of your work, and better explain how you do your work. You already have this story written—just choose the one you want to share. Base the story you'll share on your ideal target:

- What do you want them to know about you to help them choose you?

- What story illustrates what it's like to work with you?

- What do they care about and struggle with?

Don't list your job titles, clients, or abstract ideas. Tell them how you have helped others in a way that lets them imagine you doing the work. Write for one specific company or person. What story would they care about the most?

Finally, add more interest to your profile by adding a few more facts. These could include:

- Three words that represent your professional brand (I use strategy, stories, reflection)

- The three skills you most want to showcase

- One story that exemplifies these skills the best

- Experiences that have influenced the way you work

- Things you have accomplished in your career

- Education that has prepared you/qualified you for this work

- What people have said about your work

- Your personal working style

Here's how that cat-sitter might craft their complete profile:

I have been caring for and counseling cats for over ten years and I am most proud of my repeat customers. All sorts of things can happen in this seemingly uncomplicated business. But there are things you can't control. A few years ago, one of my long-term clients went away on vacation for three weeks, and unfortunately didn't buy enough food to last the third week. I called every vet office in the city until I found the cat's doctor. We were able to determine the brand, and I bought a pack of it to last until the owners came home. Over the last ten years, I have created processes that make running this business a joy. My books are full, I have repeat customers, and I spend more time with my favorite beings—cats—instead of running between appointments. I'd love to help you fill your books too. I train new cat-sitters on starting your business, marketing it to your right people, and organizing it the right way from the start. We work over a three-month period to get your business set up. We meet over the phone once a week and, by the end, most people who work with me say, "It feels like we've known each other forever." Cat-sitting can be a successful business, either as a side project or full-time operation. Do

you want to spend time with cats or on business development sites? I've spent the time on the business sites, and
I can ease the process for you and your clients.

Don't forget the call to action. If you want your ideal people
to do something, tell them what to do. A call to action can be:

- Sign up for my newsletter.
- Follow me.
- Connect with me.
- Book a free call.
- Send me a message.
- Read my book or article.

The call to action in the final line of our cat-sitter's profile
might look like this:

> If you're thinking about starting a cat-sitting business and
> don't know where to start, book a call with me here: (link).
> I promise I don't bite (unlike some of the clients I serve).

A little tip: turn *off* the broadcast updates at the bottom of
LinkedIn's profile edit page until you aren't changing your
profile as often. This prevents your network from getting
a message every time you make a change to your profile.

Research How Your Target Uses LinkedIn

Once your profile is updated, get into sleuth mode to find
out how the company or client you want to work with uses
LinkedIn. The first thing to look at is the "activity" section,

which usually appears right under their profile. If you see activity, check out:

- What kinds of things they like

- What kinds of posts they comment on, and what kind of comments they make

- Who they follow

- Who your common connections are

- What time they seem to be most active on LinkedIn

If you know what kind of content they like, you can comment intelligently on those types of posts. If you notice they like almost all of one person's posts, you can also follow that person.

Do they comment on certain types of posts? Comment on those posts too. (Remember to keep your goal and career brand in mind as you do so.) People get notifications when someone else comments on the same content. This is a way to build your voice and recognition before you reach out.

If you know who your common connections are, you can comment and like their content too (as long as you really like it). You can also ask your common connections for an introduction. If you know what time they are active on LinkedIn, you can map out your commenting and content strategies for those times.

People's behavior on LinkedIn gives you huge clues about what they like and how you can get on their radar.

It's usually best to follow them for a while before making a connection request—you'll be able to create a better request if you know more about them.

Be Intentional with Your Posts

Today, when you log on to LinkedIn, imagine that you need to prove yourself to everyone. Imagine that everyone on LinkedIn has no idea what you do, or what your value is. Try commenting or posting content with this feeling. How does it turn out? Notice how your body feels when you create and interact with desperation. People can sense it, even when it's online.

Tomorrow, when you log into LinkedIn, imagine everyone loves you. They all understand you and you know your role. You share thoughts and ideas and people are happy to hear your point of view. Content comes easily and people value your work.

Part of being successful on LinkedIn is believing in your dream. From now on, every time you go on LinkedIn, think, "I belong here. I am here to make an impact and connect with my ideal people." See how believing in the dream helps you get over yourself. You get nowhere without action.

NAIL THE INTERVIEW

You've perfected your career stories and your storytelling, you've connected with the right people, you've crafted the ideal resume, cover letter, and public profile—and guess what: you landed an interview! Congratulations! Now it's time to prepare some more.

First, gather a few things together:

- The job description
- The resume you submitted
- The names of the people who will interview you

Next, make a few notes about the goals you have for this interview (beyond landing the job):

- How did you position yourself in your resume? Match that voice and those skills.

- What skills do you want to highlight?

- What do you want them to remember about you after you leave?

- Why do you want this job?

- Why are you the perfect person to do this job? Why now?

Interviews come in different forms: there is the screening interview, the real interview, and the fit interview. Often, you'll go through all of these, in the forms of interview rounds one, two, and three. You need to prep for each one differently.

The Screening Interview

Much of the work you did to create your cover letter will prep you for this first interview. This is about showing them why you want to work for their company, why you want this specific role, what your super skills are, and some examples of your work. It's basically for HR to make sure that who you said you were on paper matches your real personality. So don't worry about "repeating" yourself by reiterating what they've already read on your cover letter and resume.

Your interviewer will likely ask you these questions:

- "Why do you want this job? Why this company?" To prep for this, simply refer to paragraph one of your cover letter.

- "What top skills do you bring to this role?" Review the second and third paragraphs of your cover letter.

- "Why are you leaving your current job?" Review the fourth and fifth paragraphs, where you tell them what you're trying to accomplish or how you're trying to grow.

Sometimes, your interviewer will ask other questions, like, "Are you experienced in (this skill)?" Be honest with your answer. You're simply confirming your career brand.

The biggest thing to remember about this interview is to add details to every answer. Tell a short story that helps your interviewer imagine you doing the work. Instead of just answering "I bring the skill of communication and organization," you could say, "I once organized a 2,000-person march in our city in under a week. I was in charge of all communication with protesters and media, and I bring that level of organization to any job." This makes the skill real for them.

If you are an entrepreneur, a client's screening interview often takes the form of a discovery call, and it will work a little differently. Do your homework and have an idea of what you're hoping to sell to the client, along with some useful advice to give them. You're the one leading the conversation.

Make notes before the call, including things like:

- What you think this person needs

- A simple tip you can give them based on your research

- A story about a previous client who had the same problem and how you helped solve it

- What questions you want to ask them

The Real Interview

The real interview might take place over the phone, online, or in person. For any one of these, you'll need to prep using the job ad and some index cards.

First, take the ad and write each line out separately on the top of its own index card—these will likely be interview questions. You can prep for an interview alone, but if you have someone who can help you rehearse your answers and assess how you're doing, that's best. Make flash cards by writing out the possible questions and answers on index cards and have your friend test you—see page 214 for an effective process you can do with your volunteer partner.

The main thing to remember is to be the same person you were in the resume that landed you the job, and to maintain the same career brand in how you present yourself and in all the stories you tell and answers you give. If you didn't use a resume to land the job, review what the person knows about you that led them to booking a meeting with you.

The Fit Interview

It's normal for a company to call you in for a fit interview after a few regular interview rounds—this is where you'll meet other employees that you might be working with. Management is looking to see if you click with everyone, so it usually has a more casual tone. In advance of the fit interview, ask who is going to be there and do some research ahead of time to help decide what stories to tell and to whom. Dress how you would dress for the job: if the workplace is business casual, go in business casual, even if you dressed in business attire for the previous interview. (Unless you'll be the leader, in which case keep it business.)

Body language is very important in this interview, and you'll want a variety of the stories you practiced in Step 8. You can share professional stories that you already used in previous interview, because these potential co-workers likely haven't heard them yet. But also prep one or two personal stories, particularly ones that are often a hit with your current co-workers. They could be related to a hobby or sport you play, but stay clear of politics and religion.

Practice telling them using the SOAR method I described on page 172.

Often in fit interviews you will meet one or two people who want to drill you and ask hard questions. Tell these people your interview stories. Others would rather be working, so they just ask regular questions about your life—of these, share your hobby and other stories. What's more important than what you're saying is the story you're telling by how you greet people, listen to them, and help them feel comfortable through open body language, eye contact, and asking clarifying questions.

ACTIVITIES TO SUPPORT STEP 10

Keystone Resume

Turn all of your career stories cards into accomplishments statements, and build out your keystone resume. If you do this work before you see an opportunity, you'll be ready to pick a format and quickly pull together a great targeted resume.

Web Presence

If you're opening a business, start working on your website. While social media is a great place to get attention, you'll also want an external landing page or shop set up. What will the domain be? How are you going to show off your personal career brand?

Social Platforms

Decide which social media channel is best for your brand and goals. Set up your profile and brainstorm what you could share.

LinkedIn Planning

Journal about what you want your LinkedIn profile to highlight. What three skills do you want to showcase? What stories showcase these skills the best? Which work experiences have influenced the way you work? How? What kinds of things have you accomplished in your career?

Interview Practice

Find a partner and practice some of your responses to possible interview questions. You can create questions from the job posting, like with the example on page 214, or you can even adapt some of the career stories prompts you'll find starting on page 296.

STEP 10 CHECK-IN

1   Do you feel you have all the marketing pieces in place to sell yourself? If your ideal company or customer was to show interest today, do you have something to send them? If not, plan when you'll make it.

2   Did you learn anything about yourself as you worked on your marketing materials? Did old voices of doubt pop

up and say something like "this is pointless" or "no one will be impressed by this"? If so, write down those doubts and give yourself three reasons why they are not true.

—

PLAN, MAKE,
AND SHARE

—

HUMANS ARE MAKERS. We forget this sometimes though, and get tricked into thinking we're only consumers. We are here to make. Even if you don't think you're inherently creative, you can still make.

The biggest skill to develop once you have career clarity is putting yourself and your work out there.

People won't tap you for incredible opportunities if they don't know what you can do. Many brilliant, kind, educated, and creative people have average careers because they don't share their awesome with the world. You're going to be different.

When you don't share your awesome with others, you're hurting them. You're hurting them by not letting them know how all of your skills and experiences could help them. It's selfish to keep it all for yourself.

If you've gotten to this step, you now have a solid career brand, fantastic marketing materials, and a network of people you can run things by. I'm asking you to take one little step more, over the line of being a viewer to being a creator.

KNOW THAT YOU HAVE SOMETHING TO SAY

My clients will often tell me, "I don't have anything to say that's new. I don't want to add to the noise." This is not true: you absolutely have something to say and a unique way to say it. Even if you're sharing information that someone else has shared, you're going to share it in a uniquely you way.

Take me, for example. I talk on LinkedIn about resume writing. I could have said, "There are already hundreds of people sharing insights about resume writing here; I'll let them do it and I'll stay quiet." But instead, I shared my ideas about resume writing. Some of what I said was brand new, and some was basic information that had been shared by others. The difference is that I shared it in my style. I gave Kerri-like examples and I showed up often enough for people to recognize how I share things.

I coached another career coach on how to show up on social media. While she and I share a lot of the same basics, we share it in our own style and voice. Her work attracts a certain kind of client, as does mine.

You can talk about a topic in your own style and it will be inherently interesting because it comes from you. If you share ideas, stories, and resources honoring your natural communication style, it will resonate with others.

BE TRUE WITH YOUR SHARING

The biggest barrier to success is pretending to be anything other than what you are. When you share, you're not seeking to be the most perfect at your work. Or the best. Don't let perfectionism stop you from moving forward. The success of your career hinges on moving out of your head and your prep materials, and into action.

A common fear is "what if my co-workers say, 'who do they think they are, posting online? Do they think they're a thought leader?'" Or, they're afraid that everyone will think they're an idiot for sharing a story. That outcome rarely happens, and even if it does, don't allow yourself to be judged by people who never take risks. They're not even on the same level as you. If you hold out to only post when your work seems perfect, you'll never deliver.

When you first share, don't compare your work to someone with a huge following. It's likely that your first few shares might not get a single like or view. That's okay; it's good, actually. It takes a few posts and interactions to get a feel for your voice. Keep on making and delivering. Keep on showing up.

The more you show up, sharing the same kind of advice, stories, and expertise, the more people will recognize you for that work. I met a friend, Jill, for coffee and I admired her nails, and I'm not usually someone who notices nails. She told me that a family friend did them for her at her house. The nail artist worked part-time as a child educational assistant during the day and painted nails a few evenings a week. I asked how I could reach her. My friend said, "Oh, she just does it for a few people and doesn't share." I said, "Tell her to start sharing photos and tagging them #nailart online." The artist listened and soon got a strong local following. She received so much demand that she connected with a local stylist, who gave her a space to work from. Over the course of one year, she was able to quit her day job and make money doing nail art. The only thing that had changed to make all this happen was that she had started to share her work and story.

IDENTIFY WHAT HOLDS YOU BACK

Before you start sharing, it's worth identifying when you have held yourself back in your career and life already. I do this exercise with clients so they can see how often they self-sabotage.

First, I have my clients think about their past and identify a time when a great opportunity came their way. It might have been a promotion, a cool project, a speaking gig, or the opportunity to contribute to a new team.

Right now, write down a few of the most incredible opportunities you have been offered, but did not take. My own examples would look like this:

1　Having a play reading in Alberta

2　Being asked to write for Thrive Global

3　Studying to be a drama therapist

4　The role of executive director of the Youth Human Rights Group

Beside each opportunity, write down what stopped you from going for it. For me it would look like this:

1   Having a play reading in Alberta—scared of it not being well received

2   Being asked to write for Thrive Global—scared my writing quality wasn't good enough

3   Studying to be a drama therapist—didn't want to inconvenience my family by moving far away

4   The role of executive director of the Youth Human Rights Group—scared that I wouldn't take the organization where it needed to go

Some situations change over time, and these barriers wouldn't stop me from taking action now. But some can still come up. List your opportunities and barriers now:

_____

_____

_____

_____

_____

_____

_____

Averting Self-Sabotage

You need a plan for when feelings of self-sabotage show up. For each reason that you use to hold yourself back from going for an opportunity in the past, write what you will do to ensure it won't happen anymore. Like this:

When I feel that my work is not high enough quality, I will _____ .

When I feel that I can't improve a project, I will

_____ .

Now, you don't have an excuse for not moving forward. To arm yourself with actions, refer back to all the work you did in Step 2 in your "Operation Manual for This Awesome Human" notebook.

When you stop yourself from taking action toward your career dreams, you're sending a message to the universe that you don't really want it. That you may like the idea of something different, but when real opportunities come to you, you'll push them away. Instead, send out the message that you value yourself, your work, and your stories. That you're ready to examine every opportunity that comes your way with your ideal work target, and take action from there.

Take a moment right now to remind yourself of your career brand and why you're ready for action today.

PLAN TO SHARE

You're about to launch your career brand publicly. You'll treat this launch the same way as any company would: you'll plan it first. It doesn't matter if you're looking to land a job or build a business—you need a plan that works with your personality.

While there are myriad online programs to help you launch your business, a common fault is that is they're based on what worked for the creator and their resources. You need a plan that works for you and your resources.

Get Clear on How You Want to Feel at Work

Take a moment to remind yourself how you want to feel at work and what kind of work you want to be doing. Remind yourself not of the specific job title, but of the way that job is going to feel. How will it be different from how your work feels now? What difference is that going to make in your life?

Plan from this place. Every time you sit down to work on your career plan, reconnect with this feeling. Why are you doing this? Why now? Write down your dream every day.

Write Down the Actions You Need to Take

You've already created all of your marketing material and made contacts in your industry, and you know what you want. But now, do you need to take a course, pass a test, or get a lower-level job in the sector before you land the big job? Do you need to get better at self-care? Do you need to save money before you launch your business? Get a piece of paper and write down all the things you need to do to land ideal work.

If you're starting a side hustle, it might look like this:

1   Decide on a business name.
2   Start sharing on social media.
3   Talk to my boss about side hustle.
4   Collaborate with Susan on the online summit.
5   Figure out what % of money to set aside for taxes.
6   Join an association.
7   Put together an offer.

If you're looking to land a job-job, it might look like this:

1   Submit my resume.
2   Write an article for LinkedIn.
3   Follow up on applications I made.
4   Prep for interviews.
5   Create a tracking system.
6   Get my references in line.

Assess Your List

Go through your list and ask yourself: "What am I capable of doing alone that doesn't drain me?" For each action that you have the skills to do, put a checkmark or a happy face. For every action that you need help with, make a note of that. Now your list looks something like this:

1   Decide on a business name. *(need help)*
2   Start sharing on social media. ☺
3   Talk to my boss about side hustle. ☺
4   Collaborate with Susan on the online summit. *(need help)*
5   Figure out what % of money to set aside for taxes. *(need help)*
6   Join an association. ☺
7   Put together an offer. ☺

Set Dates

Now you know what actions you're going to take to meet your goal. Set a timeline for these actions. If you want to land a job in six months and it's currently early March, map out what actions you'll take every month to get you to having a job by the end of August. I usually do this by working backward. For example, if I wanted to launch a new program offering at my office by August, I'd do this:

- August: Launch program
- July: Tweak communication strategy
- June: Review program results
- May: Test the program
- April: Build the program
- March: Gather data from executive team

If you're in a job search, a good timeline is four to eight weeks. In all other cases, you decide your end date.

Make a Detailed Plan for Every Month

Now, take it one step further. For every month in your plan, name the main goal and what micro-actions you'll take. List the actions that are easy, and the ones that will require you to stretch your skillset or ask for help.

For each month, make sure you're giving yourself an opportunity to use your favorite skills—this will help you build confidence in those skills, so that you're more likely to follow through. At the same time, stretch yourself a bit or do something that requires you to ask for assistance each month too. Mixing these things up will help prevent you from getting burned out in the process.

Say your best skills are in organizing, analyzing, and reporting. If you plan a whole month where you only write fluff content and attend networking events, you're going to be drained—I have seen this happen a lot. But if you add in the steps of building a tracking system and writing a research article, you're going to be using your skills to help yourself.

Assign Set Hours for Every Action

For every action you plan on taking over the next few weeks, assign a number of hours to that task and plot it in your actual day calendar. How long will it take to follow up after an interview? How long does it take you to write an article? Be generous with the amount of time you'll give yourself.

I had a client, Carla, do this. She came back and said, "But Kerri, there's not enough time to do this! I can't reach my goal because all of these tasks take too long." I told her to either extend her deadline or do less, and she said, "I want to do them all, though."

I asked Carla to go back to her tasks and her calendar and see what she could move around. After analyzing her calendar, she found she was spending six hours a month volunteering at a community organization. I asked if that volunteer role helped her reach her goals, and she said, "I joined out of guilt and I don't think I'm even helping." Carla ended up leaving the volunteer role and freeing up time to take action on her career. Her plan is to find a new place to volunteer once she reaches her goal.

This is a common issue. We over-schedule our lives, but don't make time for our dream action. We can say we're going for our dream, we can write out our dream, but if we don't make time to act on it, and be realistic about the time it takes, it's not going to happen. One of the most fail-proof ways of getting results is to be specific about when you're going to take action on your goal. These are called micro-resolutions, and they're something that Caroline Arnold wrote about in her book *Small Move, Big Change*. Your first micro-resolution can start out small, like, "I resolve to write a LinkedIn post every Thursday morning." As you follow through on the action and it becomes a habit, you can add more micro-resolutions.

REDISCOVER YOUR INNER MAKER

A big part of career growth is getting back to be being a maker—the kind of person who makes stuff. If you're applying for jobs, you'll be making resumes. You'll also make content for LinkedIn.

If you're launching your own business, you'll be making products or services. And if you're growing your career without changing it, you're likely making a new service at work or creating content to share.

I highly recommend making content to share. Never before have we lived in such an incredible time, when you can share your ideas beyond a resume or a physical meeting. You can create content that people can access without even meeting you. This gives you an opportunity to model your career brand in a way that goes further than an online profile.

If you're new to creating content, plan a mix. This can include things like:

- Resource posts (where you share a tip)
- Client success stories
- Expert posts (where you dig deep into a particular topic)
- Fun posts (ones that show your personality)

Then, go even further with other types of original content:

- Share relevant articles
- Write articles about your practice or experience

- Do a web series (I once did a #30daysofresume series, where I answered one question about resumes every day)
- Create an FAQ post or series
- Document a process
- Share a behind-the-scenes moment
- Share a big idea

What kind of content would your target like to see? Can you create something to add to that conversation?

Brainstorm some ideas and possible titles. Then, go into your calendar and mark out when you are going to post your ideas over the next month. How often you do this depends a bit on the role you have or are looking for:

- If you are an executive, I would post once or twice a week.

- If you are a manager and want to be seen as director level, post once or twice a week.

- If you want to become LinkedIn famous, post daily if you want. But note that daily posts are less attractive to hirers, so be sure posting too much won't hurt you.

If you're on LinkedIn to be seen, you'll want to bulk up on both posts and videos.

It's about playing around and testing what works for you. Once you start posting, you'll find out what resonates with your audience. And you can play the content game from there. Test with posting at different times of day and with different topics.

In addition to creating and sharing content, you also want to schedule in time to be active on LinkedIn as a social person—it is social media after all. Schedule two or three 15-minutes slots a week in which you'll comment on other people's posts. Just be sure that your comments are reflective of your career brand. It's better to leave a smart and engaging comment than to say something like "great idea." Imagine that your ideal employer or client was going to read your comment. What do you want them to think of you?

The more often you comment and share ideas, the higher your profile will rise. Plus, you're leaving a trail of great content that reinforces your career brand.

One hot tip: it's super common for people in job search to make posts on LinkedIn about what's wrong with job search. While these posts may get you a lot of likes, they don't make you look like an awesome candidate. Stick to sharing content that adds value and helps people understand how you are useful. Don't let the short-term reward of getting a lot of likes sabotage your credibility and long-term plan.

One more hot tip: sometimes people in job search get excited about the job search tips that career coaches share on LinkedIn. Remember, your purpose for being on LinkedIn is to land a job or clients. You can certainly read the tips, but it's better to avoid liking or sharing this kind of job search content when you're actively looking for a job, because doing so can make you look like a professional job seeker, rather than a professional. Stick to liking and commenting within your area of expertise. That's the way to positioning yourself as an expert who can demand higher salaries or fees.

And if you actually do this, guess what? You're now a LinkedIn content creator. And an intentional one with a plan.

Remember: once you have created your content, you need to start sharing it. Make sure that every article, every reply, every action, every video shows you highlighting at least one of the skills from your career stories cards. You are showing up as the same person you show up as at networking events and interviews. Ensure you always bring it all together.

Share stories and ideas that highlight your skills and position you for the work you want. Use industry words to help people see that you understand the sector you want to work in. You are telling different stories from different angles, but the main story and sector stay the same. This builds consistency and a brand people can know and trust.

TRACK YOUR ACTIONS

Every plan is as good as its assessment. When you take action on your goals, it's important that you track that action in some way. This helps you see that you are further ahead than you were yesterday. The truth is, we never know when things are going to change for us—and that requires abandoning some control. You can gain some of that control back by simply checking in with how your actions are or are not paying off. The trick is to track the right stuff.

Milly was leading a free video series on Instagram. Every week she hosted a live call, where she answered people's marketing questions. She had about 100 people come to her lives and they made her feel great about herself.

She was also writing articles on LinkedIn and getting about 50 likes for every post she shared. She told me, "I think I'm going to give up on LinkedIn because nothing is happening there for me." I said, "How do you know?" She based it on the numbers.

I said, "Before you completely stop writing articles, make sure it's true that nothing is happening there for you. When you get a new client, ask them how they heard about you." She agreed.

Two weeks later she said, "I think you're brilliant. They all come from LinkedIn. I was so surprised by this that I went back to former clients and asked them where they heard about me. Almost all of them said referral or LinkedIn. Only one person bought from me from Instagram efforts."

This happens a lot.

Sonia, a therapist, had curated a beautiful set of images and inspirational posts for her blog and social media. She occasionally showed pictures of herself at work, mostly behind a desk in between counseling sessions. When she tracked the numbers, she noticed that people went to her website when she posted those casual photos instead of quotes. They saw her at work. Sonia adapted her strategy to be more vulnerable and show more of herself, and her popularity rose.

It pays to track.

When you apply for jobs, you might be using two types of resumes. If one type never gets you an interview, that's a good sign to change it up. You can also track the people you have met, how you followed up with them, and what the next steps are.

CELEBRATE YOUR GROWTH

Taking action on your career takes nerve and guts. It's easy to overlook the little things when your eyes are set on landing the big client or new gig. Along the way, be sure to celebrate the little stuff. That little stuff isn't so little.

The first time you get a call for an interview is worth celebrating. Creating a plan is worth celebrating. Making it through the steps in this book is worth celebrating.

As you plot your journey and have things happen during this transition, don't forget to give yourself credit. Celebrate everything you can.

ACTIVITIES TO SUPPORT STEP 11

Planning

List all of the actions you need to take. Break them down by the hour and add them to your calendar.

Creating

Make some content to share. If you're not sure what kind of content to make, consider some of these ideas:

- What do people ask you about?
- What do you wish people asked you about?
- What do you want people to know you know?
- What is your biggest success so far? Can you share that story?
- What is something you had to overcome?
- Can you teach a common thing in your industry, but in a new way?

Conscious Expansion

Build more content from your career stories and skills. For example, my career brand is that I am helpful, solve problems, and build programs. So, I make sure that every post I write shows me being helpful, and helping to solve someone's problem. Every once in a while I talk about a program I built that helped people. What content can you share that highlights your key skills over and over again, so that your content and career brand are a match?

Tracking

Create a tracking system. Use a program of your choice to track the actions you've made. It could be tracking the number of referrals you get when you post a certain type of content, or the jobs you have applied to.

Daily Check-Ins

Reconnect with your career brand statement every day. This will remind you of your goal and your skills. Write it down three times a day. Perhaps get a journal for this work.

Immediate Action

Make two micro-resolutions. Act on them right now.

Reward

Celebrate the small wins. Choose simple ways to celebrate progress as it happens. It might be treating yourself to a new book, or to a dinner out. Write out your daily wins in a gratitude journal.

STEP 11 CHECK-IN

1   Did you plot out your actions by the hour and place them in your calendar? Were you able to do them all?

2   Through planning, creating, and sharing, did you build up any new skills? If so, what are they?

3   Is your plan going as you wanted it to? If not, what can you tweak?

A FEW
LAST WORDS

N ENDING THIS BOOK, I have a lot of hopes for you. My biggest hope is that you have learned about yourself and others, and that you have a career brand you can share with your words, voice, heart, and body. My other hope is that this process of working with stories, taking care of yourself, testing things, and then launching your career brand is a process you return to every year, or whenever you need it. I personally do the entire 11 steps once or twice a year. It's automatic to me now. I love going back to the index cards when I'm feeling out of sorts in my career. I'll write for seven days, and that helps me notice subtle changes in my preferred work. It guides my next move. It's never about memorizing a script to last for all time, but about being aware of the stories I'm telling myself about work, and the story I'm telling through my words and actions.

I believe these are the new rules for the future of work:

- Remember to take time to build mindfulness in a way that works best for you.

- Share stories. Big ones, small ones, smart ones, and silly ones.

- Determine if you're the type that lives to work or works to live, and go for roles that are appropriate for your disposition.

- Be alert, and pay attention to shifts in the company and world culture. Be aware of potential skills gaps and address them before they address you.

- Remember that work is bigger than just what you need; that, as much as possible, your work contributes to making the world a better place.

- Remember that it is far harder and more painful to do work alone. Collaborate with others to everyone's benefit.

- Don't take jobs that conflict with your values, for example by causing purposeful harm to people, animals, culture, or the environment.

- Befriend and network with people outside of your sector.

- Understand that there are multiple jobs or sectors you could thrive in. You don't need to be scared of making the wrong job choice if you base your choice on your values, skills, and ideal work culture. They can all be an adventure.

- Remember that, similar to bodies, careers come in all shapes and sizes. You are the one who gets to determine what size and shape best suits you.

Do these rules work for you? If not, what would you take away or add? Build your own rules for your future of work. I humbly encourage you to make stories a part of it too.

It's with a big heart, bushels of hope, and so much enthusiasm that I see you off. I sit in anticipation thinking of the gorgeous ways you're going to share your career stories, and I'm eager to hear about how this process worked for you. Share your story with the #careerstoriesbook hashtag. I can't wait for you to find out how awesome you are. You really are. Thank you for trusting me with the journey.

ACKNOWLEDGMENT PARTY

THERE ARE SO many incredible people in my life to be grateful for. First, I acknowledge my dad, who has passed away. Without him, there would be no book: he was a masterful storyteller, and it influenced how I saw life and made connections. None of the truly great stories he told are appropriate for a career book, but I am grateful for all of them. My dad had gorgeous blue eyes, and when he got deep into a story, fiction or non-fiction, you could see them sparkle. He knew when he had hooked you, and it delighted him. A few days before he died, I told him I was quitting my secure government job to be a full-time career coach. While his own career had been with one company, he was supportive. He told me, "If anyone can make it work, you can, Ker... and maybe you'll write a book." I did, Dad.

A huge oodle of thanks to Bernadette Jiwa, who said, "You should write a book, and check out Page Two." Thank you.

Thanks and props to Page Two for working with me on this book through a surgery and a pandemic. Your team is terrific, from the way Trena White felt like an old friend on our first call to Gabi Narsted keeping me on track. And a million and one thanks to Amanda Lewis, who saw a book in my future at the same time I did, and helped me see what I couldn't. You're practicality and magic mixed into one.

Thank you to Kristin Sherry, who invited me to contribute to the resume section in her book *YouMap*, which gave me a taste of writing for print. I love what you see in me.

Thank you to LinkedIn for naming me a Top Voice in 2018. It changed my career.

I am grateful for my children, Julia and Macy. They gave me space to write this book. On one winter day, my 17-year-old daughter was considering applying for a job and asked me what to do. I shared the career stories card exercise with her, and she was excited to write her first resume. It reminded me that everyone is still hearing that they need to be perfect to land ideal work, and it motivated me to keep writing.

I have immense gratitude for my husband, Dave, who wasn't fazed when I said I was taking time off from coaching to write a book. He brought me snacks and wine on late writing nights and allowed me to claim the creative space to do this work. All the love, shark.

Thank you to everyone who follows, likes, and supports me through social media, especially on LinkedIn. I started with zero followers and a few artsy ideas about how career management should look, and you embraced it. Thank you to Galit Ariel, Stephen de Groot, Cate Friesen, Adam Karpiak, Allen Gannett, Jon Shields, and String Nguyen for seeing something in me during the early days. Your kind likes, mentions, and collaboration helped me build a following using stories. I appreciate you.

Finally, a deep and heartful thanks to all of my clients over the last 20 years, who showed up, asked for help, and trusted their stories and my advice. Your success and action allowed me to test out the theories that became this book, and helped me see I had something worth sharing.

TOOLS & RESOURCES

CAREER STORIES PROMPTS

Here is a formula you can use if stories are not coming easily to you. Grab a few index cards and a pen and find a way to get relaxed. Think back to a time you were in flow in your career—a day you left work feeling proud of what you accomplished. A moment when you felt vibrant, alive, and thought to yourself, "I was meant to do this work." A day when you left work more energized than when you arrived. A time when you felt valued and useful.

Once you have a moment in mind, start to write down the details on your first index card. Who was there, what were you doing, how did it feel? What difference were you making?

Now, come back to this page every time you feel stuck or need inspiration, and write out your responses to a few of these prompts. Start with the general prompts relating to your moment of flow, then dive into the specific prompts for the seven skills that employers look for when hiring. These won't all apply to you, your career brand, or your ideal role, so choose the ones that do.

Prompts for Your Moments of Flow

- What was going on and how were you feeling in that moment?

- Where did this happen? What was your job title?

- What difference did you make?

- What was the biggest impact you had at each organization you worked for?

- When did you have flow at work—where it seemed that time stopped, and this flow allowed a great thing to happen?

- Think of a time you left work feeling awesome, and describe that day. The events can be teeny or huge.

Teamwork Prompts

- Write about a time you worked with a co-worker to complete a project.

- Write about a time you adjusted your schedule to help someone with a project.

- Write about a time you asked for help on a project and clearly delegated tasks to ensure the project was completed.

- Write about a time you worked with other people on a project. How did you ensure a fair distribution of work?

Social Skills Prompts

- Write about a time you made a client feel welcome. What did you do?

- Write about a time you listened to a person's concerns before giving advice.

- When have you explained a process to someone? How did you make sure to explain it so they understood?

- Have you ever stayed late to help a co-worker with a project? Write about that time.

- Write about how you contributed to the morale of the team around you.

- When did you do something that made it easy for people to feel comfortable asking you questions?

- How do you make people feel welcome?

Communication Skills Prompts

- Write about a time you used your communication skills to help a client.

- Write about a time you shared an idea for process improvement.

- Write about a time you gave a project update. Do you give immediate updates or wait until the end of the day?

- Write about a time you spoke to someone who was upset and it helped them.

- Write about a time you explained a process clearly to someone. How did you know they understood?

Accountability Prompts

- Write about the way you earned a reputation for being on time.

- Write about a time you were responsible for opening the business.

- Write about the way you show up prepared to do the work. What does that look like?

- Write about a time you arrived early to ensure everything was set up.

- Write about a time your team depended on you to be somewhere. How did that support the success of the project?

Creativity Prompts

- Write about a new program you created.

- Write about a time you improved a process.

- Sometimes it's essential that we break out of the routine way of doing things. Write about a time you were able to successfully develop a new approach.

- What was a problem that you solved in a unique or unusual way? What was the outcome? Were you satisfied with it?

- Write about a suggestion you made to improve the way job processes/operations worked. What was the result?

- What have been some of your most creative ideas?

- What innovative procedures have you developed? How did you develop them? Who was involved? Where did the ideas come from?

- Describe the most significant or creative presentation that you have had to complete.

- Describe a project or idea that was implemented primarily because of your efforts. What was your role? What was the outcome?

Adaptability Prompts

- Describe a major change that occurred in a job you held. How did you adapt to this change?

- Write about a time when you had to adjust to changes over which you had no control. How did you handle it?

- Describe a time when you felt it was necessary to modify or change your actions in order to respond to the needs of another person, or a change in policy.

- Give an example of when you conformed to a policy to which you did not agree. What was the outcome?

Time Management Prompts

- Describe a situation that required you to do a number of things at the same time. How did you handle it? What was the result?

- How do you determine priorities in scheduling your time? Give an example.

- How do you typically plan your day to manage your time effectively?

- Provide a specific example of when you used time management skills to complete a project ahead of schedule. What was the project and how did you prioritize tasks?

- Write about a time when you made a mistake on a project that caused you to lose valuable time. How did that event alter your initial plan, and how did you get the project back on track?

COMMON CAREER SKILLS

Now that you have your career stories, you can use them to understand yourself better, figure out what work is right for you, start building your marketing materials (resume and LinkedIn), or simply develop your skills further. Any of these will help your career. All of them will make it golden.

Here are some common skills you can look for in your career stories cards.

Active communication

Accounting

Accuracy

Adaptability

Analyzing

Art-making

Attention to detail

Big Data tools

Bookkeeping

Building a physical object

Building trust

Business development

Buyer engagement

Charm

Closing

Compassion

Connection

Cooperation

Creativity

Critical thinking

Customer service

Dealing with difficult
people

Dealing with stress

Decision making

Delegation

Delight

Design

Emotional intelligence

Empathy

Enthusiasm

Explaining

Follow-up

Influencing

Innovation

Leadership

Listening

Modeling

Motivating

Negotiation

Numbers processing

Patience

Persuasion

Planning

Problem solving

Project management

Proposal writing

Relatability

Reliability

Research

Setting people at ease

Strategy

Teaching

Teamwork

Time management

Tracking

Training

Understanding others

Vulnerability

Watchfulness

Wonder

COMMON CAREER VALUES

Sometimes it's easier to name your values when you see them in print. Review this list and circle your top five. This will be complemented by the work you do in Step 3.

Accuracy	Delight
Accountability	Dependability
Achievement	Determination
Adventure	Discipline
Assertiveness	Effectiveness
Authenticity	Empowerment
Authority	Energy
Autonomy	Excellence
Balance	Fairness
Beauty	Faith
Boldness	Fame
Candor	Friendship
Certainty	Fun
Challenge	Generosity
Citizenship	Giving
Commitment	Growth
Community	Happiness
Compassion	Honesty
Competency	Humor
Consistency	Improvement
Contribution	Influence
Cooperation	Inner harmony
Creativity	Joyfulness
Curiosity	Justice

Kindness	Responsibility
Knowledge	Risk
Leadership	Security
Learning	Self-respect
Love	Service
Loyalty	Significance
Mastery	Simplicity
Openness	Spirituality
Optimism	Stability
Peace	Success
Pleasure	Status
Poise	Structure
Popularity	Teamwork
Power	Thoroughness
Recognition	Timeliness
Religion	Trustworthiness
Reputation	Wealth
Respect	Wisdom

RESUME STRUCTURES

Here are a few finished examples of the four most common resume formats. Use this as a guide for where the various types of information should go, and how much detail you should go into for each section. You can adapt the formats to suit your style, but stick to clean, organized layouts and standard, common fonts.

THE REVERSE CHRONOLOGICAL RESUME

Start with one to three lines to
establish your profile statement

List jobs from most recent to oldest

Include top accomplishments
for the most recent, relevant jobs

Pat Schmidt
Anytown, MD
(000) 000-0000 | pat@fakeemail.com | linkedin.com/in/patschmidt

HUMAN RESOURCES CONSULTANT

- Enthusiastic human resources professional with over 15 years' experience **planning and implementing new initiatives** alongside management.
- Drives profit by spotting program gaps and designing programs to address them.
- Highly developed interpersonal skills and an unwavering eagerness to provide **exceptional client service** to others.

WORK EXPERIENCE

Title
Company Name   year–year

- Assisted with recruitment and selection by analyzing the position, drafting a job description, screening resumes, and creating weighted behavioral descriptive interview questions.
- Provided outplacement service to over 100 CNC operators at a large metal processing plant. Consulted with management team about the change to take place and best practices when informing and transitioning staff. Resulted in better than expected acceptance and many employees landing jobs within a few days!
- Increased revenue by 13% in six months by identifying a program gap and proposing a fix to leadership. Known for spotting opportunities. Regularly collaborated with business development team to work on proposals.
- Led monthly and one-off workshops on a variety of change management and career development topics with over 95% audience satisfaction rate.
- Stayed up to date on acts, regulations, and practices affecting human resource activities and presented them at the virtual consultant bi-weekly meetings. Created print resource guides for consultant use to inform their practices and keep us legal.
- Represented organization in remote northern First Nations community. Adapted education materials to ensure cultural relevancy and to best serve client's needs. Resulted in being trusted, and invited to attend a closed celebration.

Older or less relevant jobs can
be more brief

_____

Again, start from most recent

_____

Include digital classes, MOOCs,
and other pertinent courses or
training

_____

Don't include high school

At the end, list memberships
and/or community involvement

_____

You could add "Hobbies" too,
but be cautious as this can earn
a mixed response

_____

Title   year–year
Company Name

- Led community programs department to meet strategic goals related to five off-site programs including delivery, expansion, and revenues. Cultivated strong relationships with external community organizations. One partner said, "With the previous organization it felt like a rental, this feels like a partnership."

- Reviewed and developed the HR policy relating to performance expectations. The updated policies protected the company while providing clear direction to staff.

- Evaluated programs on multiple levels to measure learning outcomes and compliance with funder's conditions. Conducted evaluations with participants, staff, volunteers, and community executive members to take into account the experience of all stakeholders.

Community-Led Environmental Project Coordinator   year–year
Local Community Center Name

Youth Programs Coordinator   year–year
Great Art Gallery

EDUCATION

Certificate   Name of school, year
Degree   Name of school, year
Certificate   Name of school, year

MEMBERSHIPS

Association name, **Member**
Association name, **Member**

VOLUNTEER AND COMMUNITY INVOLVEMENT

Title, Organization   dates
Title, Organization   dates
Title, Organization   dates

THE FUNCTIONAL RESUME

Leave off your LinkedIn if it's not
in great shape yet

Like with reverse chronological,
tell them who you are

This variation includes a full
profile statement—you can do
this with other formats too

Share career stories to back up
your skills

Show off transferable experience
that might be hard to see from
your job titles

Organize skills by theme or area
of expertise

James Chen

Anytown, NY
000-000-0000
james@fakeemail.com

EMPLOYEE RELATIONS SPECIALIST

Human resources specialist with over 15 years' experience **executing employee relations activities** in a multi-site organization. Keen knowledge and experience **interpreting and enforcing policies**. Consistently seeks out areas to improve and takes initiative to improve processes and procedures.

✓ Saved organization $123,000 in one year by introducing performance management steps to managers working with underachieving sales reps.

✓ Successfully implemented a new electronic performance management system that replaced a paper process. Resulted in an increase of performance management reviews, reduced costs, and empowered employees to take responsibility for their own career development.

Select Accomplishments

Employee Relations Strategy Experience

- Advised managers how to follow legislation related to employee sick leave. Rehearsed scripts with managers before they spoke to employees to support their development and to give them the confidence to have difficult conversations.

- Developed documentation and process for disciplining employees. Created a 60-day support strategy that met all legislative and employment laws. Coached managers how to have tough conversations with staff to address performance gaps. Remained available to support managers and employees until the performance was improved or employee left the organization.

- Proposed return-to-work offers to employees who were away due to sickness. Guided employees about the process and necessary forms. Kept in regular contact with employees while they were on leave to help them remain connected to the organization.

Policy Development Experience

- Researched regulations and bookmarked articles for future reference. Called Employment Standards office when legislation changed to ask questions and get clarification about potential internal changes. Adapted or created new policies based on changes and connected weekly with remote HR team to share new information.

Try to hit the skills they're
looking for in the job ad

_____

Briefly list work history from
most recent to oldest

You don't need repeat your
accomplishments in this format

_____

The education section can be
brief as well

_____

- Attended strategy meetings and booked one-to-one meetings with managers at all operating sites. Continually asked *what do you need?* Advised management about restructuring and gave insider knowledge that enabled the organization to thrive through changes.

Workplace Investigation Experience

- Introduced workplace investigation procedures to ensure the policy was in place if needed. Researched trends and reports and used external network to guide the procedure. Created functional templates and processes that worked for the organization.
- Coached manager and employees how to rebuild broken communication after an incident. Communicated with manager how to manage performance in a productive and positive method, while encouraging employee how to adapt behavior in the workspace. Resulted in an improved balance and professional relationship between employees.

Employment Experience

Company   year–year
Human Resources Consultant   year(s)
Human Resources Administrator   year(s)
Another Company   year–year
Administration Supervisor   year(s)
Human Resources Administrative Assistant   year(s)
The Best Company   year–year
Administrative Assistant

Education

Bachelor of Human Resources/Industrial Relations
University/College

THE HYBRID RESUME

Format your profile statement the
same way as with the functional
or reverse chronological styles

This variation adds more detail—
a good option if you have space

This can be the same as with the
chronological format

For relevant jobs, offer detail on
your top career stories

Linda Jelly

linda@fakeemail.com ♦ Anytown, CA ♦ 000-000-0000 ♦ linkedin.com/in/lindajelly

Director of Specialty Food Production (Marshmallows)

Proactive and strategic leader who has pushed boundaries to improve operations for over 10 years. Successfully plans and executes company-wide improvements to support growth and product innovation at multiple levels. Known for identifying and coaching top talent.

- Partnered with executives to consistently elevate operations and products. Designed and implemented a new production line and organization-wide restructuring program, which resulted in significant savings and increased employee engagement.

- Developed and implemented a new marshmallow production process, which:
  - Reduced production from two weeks to one week
  - Earned our company the "top marshmallow of the year" award
  - Provided a new model for making and creating new products for the company

- Developed and maintained a good understanding of trends affecting the specialty food sector. Discussed and presented trends to executive teams to support new strategies that increased profits by 25% for the past three years.

WORK EXPERIENCE

MARSHMALLOW KINGDOM	2013–Present
Director of Production	2018–Present
Production Supervisor	2013–2018

Team Management: Built strong culture and engagement in teams across the USA and Sweden. Known for spotting and growing talent by paying attention to behavior and results. Proactively tapped employees to give them stretch roles to further develop their skills.

Operations Improvements: Led a project that we called "The Grand Poof": a productivity focused initiative to replicate the efficiency of our production line. Hosted multiple meetings to get buy-in from multiple departments to a single priority and common timeline. The Grand Poof results *yielded an 18% increase in productivity year over year in the same timeframe.*

Employee Engagement and Evaluation: Hosted annual performance evaluations for senior managers and supervisors. Identified annual performance goals and mentored employees through multiple promotions. Set and attended regular meetings at all staff levels to understand employees and identify any performance concerns.

Restructuring for Improvements: Researched inefficiencies on the production line to improve production rates and product quality following a slow but significant increase to production costs. Mapped out where positions could be merged. Brought the suggestions forward and implemented the staff reduction. Trained remaining and new employees on the revised operations, which were more stimulating and art-filled. *Resulted in an 8% year-to-date improvement on productivity.*

Relationships: Partnered with multiple external suppliers and marshmallow masters to source the best materials, at a fair price for our products. Nurtured relationships by calling suppliers, remembering important dates, and attending industry events. Known for effortlessly building trust with major partners.

Other sections can also be the
same as in the chronological
format

_____

Include education,
community involvement—
whatever is most relevant

_____

Offer as much detail as you
have room for, keeping the
focus on your skills

YUM YUM YUM YUMS   2008–2013

Production Manager   2008–2013

- Developed great partnerships with production team by taking the time to understand every role and function and modeling an open-door policy.

- Developed implementation strategy to address a higher-than-desired employee injury rate. Worked with employees to locate the most dangerous equipment, and made recommendations to replace the machine. Broke down the cost and safety benefit of equipment replacement and it was approved.

- Directed and supported production leaders in identifying and establishing plans to develop individual safety opportunities and improvements that aligned with long-range planning initiatives.

- Worked with product designers on improving lower-selling products. Selected a team of the most flexible production staff to help create small sample runs of new products. These tests built morale, while decreasing external testing costs.

- Updated the way production schedules were shared with employees to ensure maximum production at all times. Worked with employees to select their ideal months for working overtime or taking vacation. This helped employees feel heard and supported, and there was a decrease in absenteeism during production peaks.

EDUCATION AND AWARDS

Leadership Excellence Course (15-month internal course), Yum Yum Yum Yums

Top Marshmallow of the Year Award, Marshies Marsh Excellence

Undergraduate courses, Blank University

COMMUNITY INVOLVEMENT

President, United Way (food security)   2018–Present

Volunteer Usher, Midnight Theatre   2011–Present

THE NETWORKING RESUME

Keep the whole resume to one page   _____

Introduce yourself and your accomplishments
as with the more formal resume styles

Detail is only needed in the profile statement
and accomplishment sections   _____

Keep this section focused on the skills and
stories your target cares about

Stick to two or three

Keep your employment history section brief—
stick to the facts   _____

Only include relevant positions

Don't include extraneous sections (volunteering,
hobbies) unless they truly show off your skills   _____

Note at the bottom that more information is
available

Kris Thomas

Anytown, TX   kris@fakeemail.com   000-000-0000   linkedin.com/in/kristhomas

RESUME WRITER

Resume writing professional with over five years' experience helping clients land jobs with great resumes. Known for ability to translate client stories into accomplishment bullets and plan strategies that get 97% of clients an interview. Works with approachability and sense of humor.

SELECT ACCOMPLISHMENTS

- Worked with a group of 150+ IT professionals following a company restructuring. Designed and delivered resume writing workshops; provided training on how to write an IT-specific resume and how to select the stories to share. Resulted in clients feeling prepared to apply for new positions.

- Worked one-to-one with a client who was transitioning from arts sector to a corporate accounting position. Created new profile statements and selected stories that highlighted transferable skills. The client was hired by their ideal firm and thrives in the role.

- Advised client on networking strategy that gave them access to insider information. Resulted in the client landing ideal job from the hidden job market.

SELECT EMPLOYMENT HISTORY

Career Coach   2012–present
Self-Employed

Career Transition Coach   2010–2012
Fancy Times Resume

Trainer   1998–2012
Corporate Boardroom Rumble

SELECT EDUCATION AND TRAINING

Advanced Resume Writing (Professional Development Organization)
Resumes for Networking (Career Stories Consulting)
HR Certificate (Excellent College)

** More detailed resume available on request

INFORMATIONAL INTERVIEW QUESTIONS

One great way to learn more about whether a particular role, company, or sector is right for you is to connect with someone who works in that area and schedule an informational interview with them. A few examples of questions you can ask at this interview follow—but first, remember this important note: when requesting an informational interview, recognize that no one owes you this meeting, and they're doing you a favor if they agree to one. Come prepared, and respect the time limit.

The Actual Role

- What is your typical day like? Can you describe it in detail?

- How often do you work in the zone or have flow in your job?

- What does that mean to you?

- How is the actual work different than you expected it to be?

The Company

- How did you land this job?

- Is there an internal referral program?

- What skills are most desired by this company?

- What additional book or resource would help me to prepare to work here?

- Can you describe the culture of the organization?

- Do you see increased demand for this position?

- Are there catchphrases or words that you use in your team?

- Is there anyone else you think I should talk with to get more information?

- How is information shared?

The Sector

- What do you think is the biggest problem facing this industry?

- Are there any associations that I should be part of? Which is the most respected?

- I've done some research, but I'd love to know who you think are the biggest players in this sector. Also, who is rising to the top quickly? Why do think they are?

FURTHER READING

Creativity and Mindfulness

Joseph Goldstein, *The Experience of Insight*
Julia Cameron, *The Artist's Way*
Pema Chödrön, *Welcoming the Unwelcome*

Storytelling and Writing

Bernadette Jiwa, *Story Driven*

Bobette Buster, *Do Story*

Clem Martini, *The Blunt Playwright*

Money

Tiffany Aliche, thebudgetnista.com

Vicki Robin, *Your Money or Your Life*

Yes & Yes, school.yesandyes.org

Business

Michael Schrage, *Who Do You Want Your Customers to Become?*

Paul Jarvis, *Company of One*

Seth Godin, *This Is Marketing*

Job Search and Careers

David Burkus, *Friend of a Friend*

Dev Aujla, *50 Ways to Get a Job*

Dorie Clark, *Stand Out*

Herminia Ibarra, *Act Like a Leader, Think Like a Leader*

Laura Huang, *Edge*

Roman Krznaric, *How to Find Fulfilling Work*

INDEX

target, 124; COVID-19 pandemic and, 97–98; within current job, 107–8; with external companies, 108; future of work and, 98–99, 104–5; self-assessment, 121–22; side gigs, 109–11; ten possible selves exercise, 99–105, 114–15; time length for, 94–96

fear, 152–53
feelings, from work, 13, 88–89, 269
first impressions, 187–88. *See also* greetings; introductions
fit, 73–89; introduction, 73–75; activities to support, 86–89; check-in, 89; fit interview, 257–58; formula for defining, 82–83; importance of, 75–76; losing work due to, 73–74; management/reporting style and, 78–79; people and, 76–78, 86–87; spirituality and, 83–86, 89; work environment and, 80–81, 88–89; work style and, 80
flow, career stories prompts, 296
follow-ups, in networking, 196–97
freelancing, 108. *See also* entrepreneurs; side gigs
frustration, 148

functional resume format, 224–25, 234, 308–11

gist, 240
graphic resume format, 228
gratitude journaling, 49, 281
greetings, 177–78. *See also* first impressions; introductions
growth: celebrating growth, 279, 281; growth fever, 62–63; growth targets, 123–25

handwriting, 12
header, on resumes, 229–30
heroes exercise, career, 111–14, 116
hybrid resume format, 225–26, 234, 312–15

Ibarra, Herminia: *Working Identity*, 99
"I love myself" meditation, 41–43
industry struggles, 135
industry terminology, 130–33; introduction, 130–31; business words, 132; entrepreneurial words, 133; soft and slang words, 133; technical words, 131–32
informational interviews, 108, 318–19
intentions exercise, 154
internal stories, 35

ABOUT THE AUTHOR

KERRI TWIGG IS the founder and operator of Career Stories. Through courses and coaching, she helps people use their stories to grow their careers, whether they aim for a "job-job" or running their own business. And if they're not even sure yet what kind of work they're aiming for, she helps with that too. Kerri has been helping people find and share their stories with confidence for nearly 20 years, seven of those in the career management sector. For individual clients, she guides them into discovering what makes them awesome, and shows them how to use that awesome self to direct their career; for businesses, she supports them as they restructure or downsize, and helps employees manage change or job loss. You can find out more about Kerri at career-stories.com.

CPSIA information can be obtained
at www.ICGtesting.com
Printed in the USA
BVHW070950250121
598676BV00001B/202

9 781774 580615